Dandelion Wishes

The Untold Story of Coral Maxwell-King

Lisa King

Felen Press

Copyright © 2023 by Lisa King

All rights reserved.

No portion of this book may be reproduced in any form without written permission from the publisher or author, except as permitted by copyright law.

ISBN – 978-0-6483026-8-1 (Paperback)
ISBN – 987-0-6483026-9-8 (Large Print)
ISBN – 978-0-6482036-7-4 (eBook)

A catalogue record for this book is available from the National Library of Australia

Contents

Dedication	V
Preface	VII
Fitzroy 1940	5
Parkville 1940	13
Carlton 1940	31
Parkville II 1942	73
East Kew 1943	89
Jeetho 1946	131
Mt Evelyn 1946	161
Spring House 1947	185
City Mission 1948	207
Nhill 1948	241
City Mission 1949	269
Ascot Vale 1949	283
To The Future 1949	333
Afterword	345

Acknowledgements	351
About The Author	359
Also By	363

'*Dandelion Wishes*' is dedicated to Coral, the magnificent woman we were privileged to know as 'Mum', and to all the courageous mothers whose hearts ache eternally for their forfeited, but never forgotten, children.

Dear Reader,

Writing about history is fraught with difficulties, particularly in the sensitive area of child welfare.

Every experience within the system is unique and powerful. This book does not seek to invalidate the experiences of others in the state care, and acknowledges the personal atrocities experienced by children placed within the welfare system.

This section of Coral's life takes place between the years of 1940 – 1950. Times were different then; personally, socially, politically, and economically. My aim is to remain faithful to the era, using common vernacular and grammar, and not softening personal descriptions, or common social practices.
Deception, accusations, and punishments were common, and it is easy to stand at a distance and condemn society for not doing better. The

problem with that viewpoint is many were doing the best with what they knew, just as we are today.

If we truly believe in a progressive society, we can only hope that our descendants will be shaking their heads in 80 years time and saying, 'they did *what* in 2023?'

Apart from Coral's family members, all names and physical descriptions have been changed.

My earnest hope is that through Coral's story, you might discover that not only is the truth stranger, it is often *mightier* than fiction.

Lisa King
May 15, 2023

Dandelion Wishes

Anguish flared to life deep within Coral's belly the moment Miss Staines prised Rodney from her arms. It swept to her chest stinging and scorching, as the woman sat smugly in the car and then rose further with the doff of the man's hat and the slam of the car door.

The engine growled and Coral was sure she'd never breathe again. Invisible hands formed around her throat and squeezed, compressing the pain into her chest until she thought it would burst into a million pieces.

'*Rose was right,*' Coral tried to speak, but the invisible hands made sure she remained lifeless and mute. '*They take a piece of your heart. Scoop it out, so all you feel is hollow. And then you find you're doing things you never said you'd do, ever. Things you promised to yourself and to your baby.*

Like saying goodbye.

Like sending them away.

How is it possible I'm doing the one thing I said I'd never do in my life?'

Fitzroy
1940

<u>Friday 15th March, 1940—Victoria Parade, Fitzroy</u>

"Shit!"

Albert Maxwell tumbled through the darkened doorway, his runaway momentum stopping just short of the rattled hall table. Delia Snelling jumped to the defence of her favourite vase and captured her prize just as it toppled to the floor.

"Shh Bert! For goodness sake." Her frown burrowed a familiar line across her forehead, "This boarding house is one rescue mission after another." With her precious ornament secured in place, she raised one side of her mouth while Bert found his feet.

"It's not grog, honest!" he whispered, "I'm just stuffed[1] Mrs Snelling, that's all."

He opened his mouth wide and offered her to confirm his assertions.

"I think not, Mr Maxwell."

Bert raised calloused hands and stepped gingerly around the hall table; his voice barely discernible. "Sorry Mrs Snelling … kids asleep?"

"You've missed them again," she nodded. "Your tea's in the oven."

Bert's face filled most of the little shaving cabinet mirror. He jumped his hands between the cold and hot tap, but no matter how much he scrubbed

---

1. Tired

with the bar of Solvol[2], that dirt wasn't coming off. Who'd have thought it'd be so hard to get rid of Sunbury? He snorted at his reflection just as a welcoming thud from the kitchen table announced his tea was ready. It wasn't a hard sound, Mrs Snelling was always sure to lay that bloody lace tablecloth out every time they ate. Don't know why she bothered. A 'fine' house is not something you'd ever find in Fitzroy. She probably had one of those fine homes once, but that was before the depression, and now the war. He shrugged at his reflection. A lot of men come home to worse. Particularly these days.

The meat was stringy, and the mashed potatoes had formed a chewy crust. Bert didn't mind. It was his usual Friday fare and the price he paid for being late. He bet the kids said it was delicious, though. His landlady wasn't about to cook another meal just for him. Mrs Delia Snelling was many things, but a practical woman was at the top of the list. Well, except for the damn lace tablecloth that kept catching on his rough hands. She wouldn't be moved though. Once she made her mind up, that was it. He moved the dry food around in his mouth and imagined what it was like before its stint in the oven.

"Take the long way 'round again, did they?"
Albert chewed and swallowed the meat before it was ready. "Tommy's missus wasn't well, so the truck went over to Coburg first, then it came back this way."
"I see."
Something was troubling the old girl. She'd tied the back of her apron around her plump frame and then fixed it again three times before preparing the teapot. Bert grimaced. It'll be cups of tea for most of the weekend. Once back at camp, he'd knock a few or more back with the boys. The forestry camp was tough work, but without it, there'd be no sustenance payments.

---

2. Ground pumicestone soap bar

Bert leant over the newspaper, fork halfway to his mouth. War reports covered most of the front page. Maybe something in the paper triggered her off? The teapot settled on the table and Mrs Snelling gently turned it three times before she reached for the teacups in the cupboard. Bert shook the newspaper straight in his hands. "Each to their own I say, but I don't get how these larrikins on the wharf can be on strike, jeopardising their jobs, when I can't even find one to earn a decent pound for my lodgings."

"We all have our own battles and injustices to deal with Mr Maxwell." Mrs Snelling inspected her cups without a glance at Bert.

"True enough, Mrs."

The older lady poured their tea and took two slices of apple pie from the warmer.

Bert folded and tossed the crumpled paper onto the table in a flash. "What, sweets too? Now this is a treat. Delia, your blood's worth bottlin'[3] the things you do for me."

"Well, it was you who reached those top branches. There wouldn't be extra pie without your help. The children enjoyed it."

"I'm sure they did."

"I kept mine to eat with you, as I have some news, Albert. And I thought a meal together would be a fitting time."

Delia followed her hands as they spread over the lace tablecloth and spoke without looking at him. "Remember how I told you I didn't want my home to become a boarding house after George died? Didn't want all these people coming and going. But you adjust when life deals you a terrible blow, don't you?" She glanced at Bert to confirm his attention before moving on. "Often in ways and in means you're sure you won't adjust to, but you do. You do." She nodded to herself and sipped at her tea. "You stand back up and ask yourself, 'Delia, what's the next step?' That's exactly what I did. If I wanted to keep the house; I needed to open it up as a boarding house. Hmmm." She agreed with herself, "Hide the silver; open up."

---

3. You're wonderful.

"I like that one," Bert chuckled. "Hide the silver, open up. I might not have silver to offer you Mrs Snelling, but at least my susso work provides enough to keep me and the kids here; we're very grateful."

"My mother is very ill, Albert."

Bert leant his forearms on the table, unsure of how familiar he should be at such a time. "Oh, I'm sorry to hear that."

"I have to go and tend to her,"

"Of course…"

"In Mansfield."

A lump developed in Albert's throat. He sipped nervously, but the tea wouldn't wash it away.

"My brother; he married a Polish girl after the Great War. Beautiful couple. He fell ill shortly after their arrival back in Australia and we lost him a month ago. Tuberculosis, you see."

Albert nodded; grateful he didn't need to speak.

"It's not the life she expected, poor Anna, nor the one she wanted, but today is not the day to argue with God about such matters. Some things just are, and railing about them does nothing to ease the day. Today's question is not about *why*, or *woe is me*, but to rise from the blow and ask 'what's the next step?' That's the predicament Anna finds herself in. And now, dear Albert, the predicament you find yourself in."

Bert's voice was dry. "Me? Why?"

"Anna has agreed to run the boarding house while I tend to my mother. Daughters are closer than daughters-in-law, particularly in times of illness, you see, and I must look after my own interests and keep the house running. You do understand, don't you?"

"Of course, Mrs Snelling, and I'm sure I'll like her. She sounds… resilient."

"No. There's a problem."

"A problem?"

"She doesn't '*do*' children, Bert. There won't be anyone to tend the children while you are away at the Forestry Camp."

The lump was back. Thick and dry and strangling.

"She is firm about that. The poor dear has had enough troubles this year and as she's doing me a favour, I don't feel right to complain."

"Right then." Bert stood and paced the linoleum floor, rubbing his hands through his dark hair.

Mrs Snelling had twisted her handkerchief into a ball. "You could always try to find another boarding house that might accommodate the children."

"It was hard enough to find you here. I'm at a loss. I never thought I'd be 36 and desperate for a roof over *my* head, let alone for my three kids."

Bert paced while Mrs Snelling poured more tea. She rose to get the Bex[4], and lifted the familiar blue and yellow box toward him in offer. He nodded. All the pubs were closed, and he'd need something to help him sleep later. For now, he just needed to keep moving. Moving and thinking.

Mrs Snelling sipped at her Bex laden tea. "There are some scenarios, I expect, that might help you with your decision. You could take them out on the streets and see how you all fare, but no, I really can't see you doing that. Perhaps you could find someone to leave them with, but then you've already exhausted all your options, or you wouldn't have ended up here."

Bert shook his head and continued to pace. Mrs Snelling wrung her hanky and her shoulders softened; then drooped. Poor old love, must be the early effects of the Bex. What he really needed was some scotch.

Her voice broke through his thoughts. "It's not anyone's fault. It's life, and life deals us all terrible blows at times. I'm sorry I can't offer any more suggestions." She rose from the table, patted his arm, and motioned to his tea before she left to retire. "Well, you know what? Anna won't be here until Wednesday. That gives you a few days for this news to knock you down, and for you to get back up, and ask yourself, what's next?" She tried to give a comforting smile, but the smiles they offered each other were just dismal reflections. "I'll be leaving on the Thursday morning train."

"Shit!" The word came out louder than expected.

"Rail for only a small while, Mr Maxwell. Then ask, what should I do next?"

---

4. A CPA based analgesic in powder form

Did he nod? He felt he did.

Mrs Snelling wandered the darkened hallway to her room at the front of the house.

Good ol' Delia, her big heart had extended far enough. He didn't begrudge her a thing.

She didn't even have to mention *what* was next. In this day and age, every man and his dog knew what was next.

There was enough of it everywhere.

Parkville

1940

<u>Monday 18th March, 1940—Royal Park Depot, Parkville</u>

It was sunny when they left home. The elm trees along Victoria Parade had begun their colourful march toward autumn, and the crisp morning made their yellows seem sharper. It wouldn't be long until they'd be playing in the refuse, giggling and kicking the fallen leaves into the air.

Three-year-old Ronald wriggled and squirmed his hand inside Coral's. She tried squeezing it, tugging it, but nothing worked. "Da-aad, Ronald won't stop fidgeting."

"Here, you take my hand, Ronald. Coral, you hold on to Allan's."

Everyone settled, and they stepped out, Coral and Allan in the front, Dad and Ronald behind.

Coral sighed when they turned into Nicholson Street; it stretched in front of them like it went on forever.

"Where are we going again, Dad?"

"To see a lady."

"Do we have to walk *all* the way to the city?"

"C'mon, we've done it before."

It was true. They once walked to the city to see the light on top of the T & G building and Dad carried them home in Mrs Snelling's wheeled shopping basket. She always wondered how it got that funny bulge in it, but no one ever told.

Coral squished her feet up inside her shoes, but her toes still hurt. Mrs Snelling helped dress the children; fussed over washing their faces, and insisted Coral wore the shoes with the little flower on the top.

"But I like my comfy black ones."

"I know dear, but look how they're scuffed and broken. They just will not do."

"Won't do what?" Coral asked, but Mrs Snelling just gave them longer hugs than usual, told them to be good, and sent them on their walk to the city. Dad said Mrs Snelling's mum was sick. That must be why she looked so sad.

Each time Coral looked at Dad, he smiled at her, but she caught just as many glances of a strange sadness etched on his face. It must be that kind of day. The city was grey, and paper blew in the streets. Even though it was sunny, the cold air ran straight up the street *'as straight as a tram'* like Dad said. A fresh gust made the trees wave. Dad held on to his hat, and Coral pulled her cardigan closer. She was glad she'd done up all the buttons before they left. Except for the one missing near the top that she'd never noticed until the cold tickled its way around her neck.

Halfway down Nicholson Street, Dad and Coral took turns to carry Ronald, and Allan tried hard not to whine, but he was never as good at pretending as Coral. He got a magical second wind at Parliament House.

"Look at all the steps! I'm gonna climb to the top!"

He ran all the way up and then slowly stepped his way back. While they waited, Coral pulled a dandelion from a crack in the footpath. It was perfectly round and not one seed fell as she plucked it and brought it to her mouth.

"Do you know what they do here, love?"

Coral shook her head, and let her breath slink away. She'd have to wait for Dad to finish too.

"They make laws. The ones that affect us all, whether we like them or not."

Allan jumped the last step and landed with both feet on the concrete. "I'd make a law that you had to eat ice-cream for tea!"

"What about you Coral?"

"That all shoes have to be comfy." She blew hard at the dandelion, and waited with her eyes closed, but her toes still felt like they were on fire.

Ronald contributed with a grin and a shout of "Ice Cream!"

Dad scanned the street. "You beauty! Right on time. Quick, hold hands!"

They crossed into the middle of the road like a wayward piece of string, with little Ronald's legs bringing up the rear. While the children were eager to cross to the other side of the road, Dad held them back.

He looked further back up the street, "Here's a treat then."

Ding! Ding!

Ronald's mouth dropped open and Allan jumped up and down on the spot. A tram ride! Allan scrambled inside and knelt on the slatted board seats and Ronald giggled with every ding of the bell. At each stop and start, Coral wondered about the people getting on and off and what they were up to that day. Dad swung between laughter and sadness. He wasn't himself at all today, but then again, all the grownups were strange lately. Must be the war stuff they all keep talking about. Soon enough, he stood to tug on the cord.

"Here's our stop!"

"Aww," three little voices complained as one.

Dad scooped Ronald up, and Allan and Coral held hands and clambered from the tram and across to the footpath.

"More walking?" Allan asked.

"Just a short walk now."

"Promise?"

"Promise."

Dad held his hat in his hands.

"Well, here we are."

It was a funny looking building. Big and made of red brick, but it wasn't a school, and it didn't look like the offices in the city either.

Once inside the heavy door, Dad arranged them in a line across the wall. "Stay there. Be good now."

It was like a bank inside, with a big, long counter that separated the workers from the normal people.

Allan nudged Coral, "That's the same lady that came to our place yesterday."

"Shh Allan." But it *was* her. The short lady with the round middle and her hair in a bun at the back of her head. Her suit looked most important, just like it did yesterday when she sat at the kitchen table and had a cup of tea with Dad. There were lots of papers and Dad wasn't cheery at all. Why have we come to see her again if dad didn't like her?

The lady with the bun looked across the counter at the children, and Coral smiled. She didn't smile back. *Mrs Dawson.* That's what Dad said her name was.

They were still standing to attention when Dad returned. He kissed Ronald and Allan's heads and kissed Coral on the cheek.

"You'll be a good girl, won't you?"

Coral frowned, and a lump formed in her throat. "Yes, Dad." Allan was close enough to shove with her shoulder. "What about you Allan?"

"Yes, Dad."

Ronald moved behind them and hung onto Coral's leg.

"I'll be back soon. They'll take care of you here. It's better that you're here for a little while."

The lump in Coral's throat burst into a gasp, and tears welled in her eyes. *You're leaving us here with the lady? Why? What did we do?*

"It'll be alright love. It's like Mrs Snelling said, life's just tough sometimes, and you must do what you think is best. It's only for a little while, alright? You sit here. I'll be back soon."

Coral sat between the boys on the hard wooden bench, held their hands, and strained to hear what the people behind the long counter were saying.

The lady with the round tummy held papers and spoke to the others behind their desks. They wrote things down sometimes, but mostly they just nodded their heads.

"Yes, yes, a boarding house. They had one room, one bed. Such a small room too, unkempt, and unhealthy for the children. He's quite unable to care for them."

"Mmm, quite," one said.

"You've recommended they be committed to state care, then?"

"Well, they can't be on the streets."

"Heavens, no."

Mrs Dawson strode around to their side of the counter, clipboard in hand. She ran her finger down the side of the paper.

"Hello Coral, it says here you're nine years old."

"Yes."

"Allan, you're six and little Ronald here is three."

"Yes, that's right," Coral said.

Two women came, took the boys' hands, and led them away.

"But…" Coral lunged for them, but Mrs Dawson stood in her way.

"The boys go over there," she explained as they disappeared behind a big swinging door.

"But I…" and the boys were gone before she could remind them to be good, and most importantly, that Dad said it was only for a little while, and that he'd be back soon.

The bathtub was warmish. Not cold, but not comforting either, not like Mrs Snelling's tub.

"Seems healthy and tidy." The lady wrote her words down on some papers.

"Oh, there's lice here," said the other, accompanied by more scribbling.

Mrs Dawson left her in the care of these two women who stripped her and plonked her in the bathtub without even asking her name.

Coral watched little bubbles form on the surface of the greyish water. It smelt like pine. Like the stuff Mrs Snelling washes her floors with. And for a while she imagined she had shrunk and was sitting in Mrs Snelling's mopping bucket.

Ugh! Whatever they put on her head was cold, and it stank. Bleah! What *was* that smell? She knew it from somewhere. The mop bucket smelled nicer, and the pine was still there, somewhere under the acrid stink of the stuff that was dripping down the sides of her face. It's the lamp oil! The stuff Dad put in the lamp to go to the outhouse! Her eyes slammed shut, and she tried to hold her breath and keep her head still while they scrubbed it into her hair.

"Do we know this one's story?"

"The father's agreed to send money to help with their care. Mother left 18 months before. They don't know where she is; took off with another man when this little one was eight. The youngest, a boy, is about three now, probably won't remember his mum at all."

"Well, that sounds fortunate, given their circumstances."

"Their dad was working in sustenance camps out at Sunbury."

"That's a long way out. What happened to the kids while he was gone?"

"That's the whole point, isn't it?"

"At least it's another soul out of those Fitzroy slums. And early enough that they're not stained by such hard living."

The bath water was cold and grey, and the stink had taken over the pine completely. Coral rubbed her arms in a hug, but the water had made her hands too cold and clammy to offer any comfort.

It wasn't sunny anymore. Clouds covered the sky all afternoon and stayed until Coral couldn't see the sky anymore.

"Lights out!" a voice called, and the room grew dim. It took a while for her eyes to adjust, but the streetlights along Parkville Road still crept some of their light in behind the curtains. What an enormous bedroom. Coral counted the beds; ten on this side, and ten on the other. All the same; all with grey blankets and white sheets with little bodies inside. Some tossed and turned, making the springs creak, some sobbed quietly, and some curled in little grey wool balls at the ends of their beds.

Coral didn't feel like crying. She didn't feel like anything.

Her hands felt around in the sheets. They were starchy and stiffer than the ones at home. And empty. There were no brothers to cuddle into to keep warm, no snoring dad, and no funny farts to giggle at. Coral waved her hands around her face, but it still smelt like she had a cloud of kero[1] around her. She pulled her blanket up around her shoulder and snuggled into the cold pillow.

It's okay, dad said it's only for a little while.

'Soon' was one of those funny words grown-ups use.
"Mum'll be here *soon*." That's what he said.
"Things'll get better *soon*."
"I'll have more money *soon*."
"We'll move out of this small room *soon*."
"Y'know, when things are a bit better."
That kind of soon seems to take forever.

But sometimes 'soon' came quicker than you thought it would. Like 'It'll be morning soon', or when you're playing in the street, and it feels like you've hardly played at all, and you have to come in soon.

At first, Coral thought Dad's 'soon' meant *soon*, like when he went to the pub and was home in time for tea.
Maybe his soon meant when the sun went down.
Soon didn't mean bedtime either.
Soon was one of those words grown-ups use, to mean whatever they want it to mean.

---

1. Kerosene

Soon didn't mean when the sun came up either.

Or at breakfast time when she was jostled along a long table and ate weetbix and milk with more girls than she'd ever seen in one place before. Big ones and little ones, loud ones, and quiet ones.

"What day is it?" she asked the girl next to her.
"Thursday."
"Already? I thought it was Wednesday."
"Nope. Thursday." Weetbix nearly fell out of the girl's mouth as she spoke. "Hope you're ready for the spelling test today."

School went by in a blur, just as the days did. The classrooms were in the only white building on the grounds, and it was already cold in there, even in March. Miss Johns was a nice enough teacher, but she was often tired and unwell. The other grown-ups who took her place when she was ill were much worse. Coral made up a game and tried each day to see if she could avoid every angry grown-up in the whole place. Especially the ones who yelled and lashed out at the other children and called them horrible names and made them do awful chores on top of their normal afternoon ones. She tried, but wasn't always successful.

Coral played sometimes too, with the other girls when they had some free time. Sometimes she'd laugh, and then feel guilty for it. Where were the boys, and why wouldn't the grown-ups tell her anything? It was always, *'We'll see'*, or *'Maybe tomorrow'*, or even *'Shut up about it, would you?'*

Each night, she'd say her prayers, just like they told her to, on her knees beside her bed. Her hands clenched so hard her knuckles went white. Alice Porter told her if you clench your hands tight, it makes your prayers stronger. So she'd squeeze with all her might and pray that Dad would come back and get her and the boys, and they could all go to Sunbury–wherever that was. Then they'd all be together again.

Her sheets were always cold when she climbed into bed afterwards. She rubbed at her knees. The floors were cold too. Under the covers, her hands swept all over the sheets, as if by magic a brother might appear, but they never did.

The boys must still be on the other side of that big swinging door. Dad said to be good. If I'm extra extra good, maybe they'll let me see them tomorrow.

Miss Griggs' shadow passed the open door in the hallway. Coral could tell it was her because she walked so softly. She quietly poked her head around the corner and entered the dark room, pulling blankets up on sleeping children, and saying quiet prayers for others. Coral liked her very much. So much more than the other grumpy and mean grown-ups.

She caught Coral's eye as she pulled the blanket up near her chin. "It's freezing here, Miss Griggs."

"I know," she whispered, "My hands are freezing too, see? Now tuck yourself up."

Miss Griggs rubbed Coral's back until she could feel some warmth and felt sleepy.

"When can I go home?" she mumbled.

"You might not go home right away. What usually happens is someone will take you into their home."

"Not mine? Not with Mrs Snelling?"

"No, theirs, and they'll take care of you for a while."

"It'll be warmer there?"

"Oh, yes. Much warmer."

"When can I go?"

"Remember to be good now, so there are no complaints. Mrs Dawson has to go to court for you."

"What's court?"

"A place where grown-ups decide about where you should live."

"Does it matter what I want?"

"No love, as a matter of fact, for now, it doesn't. I'll let you know what's going on if I hear anything. Shh now, time for sleep."

"Miss Griggs, will my dad come back?"
"What did he tell you?"
"That it'll be better to be here for a little while."
"Well, there you go."

<u>Saturday 23rd March, 1940—Royal Park Depot, Parkville</u>

Every school day was the same, and every girl's life at the Depot was the same too.

Coral woke and aired her bed, ate breakfast, made her bed, went to school, ate lunch, played a bit, did chores, ate dinner, did some more chores, said her prayers, and went to bed. All while avoiding, as best she could, the cranky grown-ups.

Sometimes the kids had no way to avoid them, or no way to keep them happy. Coral jammed her fingers in her ears so she couldn't hear them getting the cane or being strapped, and when it got really bad, she hummed as well. *Be a good girl, Coral.* That's what Dad said.

But Saturdays were different. Not better. Just different.

The older girls led the way carrying large jam tins filled with runny floor polish and splashed small blobs of it onto the floor with a stick.

Coral and the younger girls followed behind them on their knees with polishing rags. They rubbed and cleaned and polished the floors from one end of the dormitory to the other. Other children cleaned the bedside tables, window ledges, and anything else that held dust.

It always felt good to be finished, but her knees hurt like billyoh[2]. Two of the older girls leant against the wall, tired, but with happier knees than Coral.

"It'd be nice, wouldn't it, just once?" one said.

"Just once what?" asked the other.

"I dunno. A 'thank you'. Maybe a 'good job'."

"You won't be gettin' that 'round here."

"I know. They're too busy reminding us we're the dregs of society and nobody wants us."

"Come now," the older girl said in a fancy voice, "We are merely trying to create industrious hard-working citizens of the future."

"Yeah, shut up and do as you're told, more like it."

The girls laughed the same sad laugh lots of kids had at the Depot, and when the lunch bell rang through the halls they sauntered off.

Coral stood holding her polishing rag. *Indust-rulluss what?*

An arm came from nowhere, grabbed hers and bolted past "It's Susan! Susan's coming!" Coral dropped the rag and raced down the hallway with her friend.

When Susan O'Keefe got angry, she really flipped her lid. She'd hit and bite, and she could bite *hard*. When she got upset, everyone scattered, as far and as fast as they could. It didn't take too long to learn to run, yet some were smarter than others. Susan was definitely going to get the strap again.

They arrived in the lunchroom puffing. There was no sign of Susan, but Tilly Rasmussen waved at them. She was one of Coral's favourites - maybe everyone's favourite. Tilly was only seven, but when she laughed, she sounded like a donkey. The girls did everything they could to make her giggle because it made laughter spread like a bushfire and everyone felt so good afterwards. Even the grown-ups.

Yet some girls didn't laugh. Maybe they never would. But if anyone could make them, it'd be Tilly Rasmussen.

---

2. An unimaginably large amount.

Saturday 6th April, 1940—Royal Park Depot, Parkville

"Lights out."

Warm days or cold days didn't make any difference to Coral's aching knees. She'd polished the floor three times now. Three Saturdays. The older girls said it would get easier, but it didn't! Meanies. Coral pouted and rubbed at her knees under the blankets, the warmth made them feel a little better.

Miss Griggs was halfway across the room before Coral noticed her. She looked so kind in the light, praying for Susan to stop biting and hitting, and whispering to God that she wondered what would become of her.

Miss Griggs often got in trouble for checking on the girls. *Fancy that. Getting in trouble for being nice.* Coral missed their talks, and liked to think that when she'd missed her, she was praying at the foot of her bed.

Miss Griggs tucked her in and whispered in her ear. "Do you know what Mrs Dawson did yesterday?"

Coral shook her head.

"She went to court."

"So, I can leave now and go to someone's warm home?"

"Not just yet. Now we must wait to find someone suitable."

"Suitable?"

"Miss Griggs!" They both jumped in their skin. Mrs Silcock's whisper sounded like a shout and Miss Griggs hurried out to the hallway, where more whispers that sounded like shouts occurred.

"Soo-tee-bull." Coral whispered the word under her blanket as though it might float away outside of its covering. They must have to be wearing a suit then. There were lots of people that wear suits. She'd seen them in the city. There were so many to choose from; they'd find one lickety-split[3].

---

3. Very fast

Friday 17th May, 1940—Royal Park Depot, Parkville

"Coral Maxwell!" It was Mrs Silcock, only this time she wasn't whispering. "Come with me!" Her fingers dug into Coral's shoulder and rushed her down the corridor so fast her legs couldn't keep up. Coral's heart thumped and she tilted herself one shoulder up, and one down to stay balanced.

Mrs Silcock's pace eased as they arrived in the office area, and she directed Coral into a room on the left. It looked a bit like a storage room with shelves everywhere. A lady sat on her knees on the carpet, surrounded by boxes of clothes. Mrs Silcock was gone.

"Now dear," the lady on the floor said, "You're off to Mrs Reynold's today. She has a lovely home and a lovely family in a place called Carlton. Let's get ourselves dressed then."

The lady chose a dress and tights for Coral to put on, and helped push her arms into the thick knitted cardigan.

"These shoes are a little too big, aren't they?" the lady said as she tied the laces, "Better than being too small,"

"It's Friday today, isn't it?"

"Mhmm. Why do you ask?"

"It's nothing."

Saturday would have marked her seventh turn of scrubbing the floors. She wiggled the muscles around her kneecaps, up and down and up and down as the lady brushed her hair and attached a pretty hair clip with daisies on it.

Everyone in the office looked up when Coral entered. The hard wooden seats were still there, and the big swinging solid door was closed. A new lady stood in front of her in a fitted floral dress and a thin matching belt. She had a nice hat on, with yellow flowers around its band, and soft light brown gloves.

"Coral, say hello to Mrs Reynold."

Coral looked at her shoes. "Hello."

There were a million questions in her head. She wanted to know if her house was warm and if they lit the fire at night and if she had to scrub her floors. She didn't know where Carlton was, but she was sure she'd heard someone talk about it once. But her mouth was closed shut, like someone had used the glue for the broken chairs on her lips.

The lady from the storage room pushed her forward a little. Coral gasped, lost her balance, and took a step towards Mrs Reynold, but stopped short. She wanted to go to the lady with the warm house, but her legs wouldn't move, and she felt like the sheets from her bed were twisted all around her.

"Do you like baking Coral?" Mrs. Reynold's voice was soft and kind. "I love to bake cakes and biscuits. Perhaps you'd like to help me?"

Coral wiggled her toes inside the too-big shoes. Mum didn't bake cakes and dad wouldn't know how to. Sometimes Mrs Snelling made apple pies, but not that often, and she wouldn't let them help.

"You mean I could bake a cake?" One step after another, Coral's legs found their way to Mrs Reynold. "When we've finished, can we bring some back for the others?"

"Perhaps not today, dear. You'll be too busy settling into your new home."

Goodbye Parkville

Children's Welfare Department
Secretary's Office
Flinders Street Railway Buildings
17.05.1940

Received from the Secretary of the Children's Welfare Department, the child—female—named in the margin (Maxwell, Coral 13.9.30) in good health. Boarding out with outfit.

Signed,
Mrs. E. Reynold
Rathdowne St
Carlton

Carlton

1940

Friday 17th May, 1940—Rathdowne St, Carlton

The taxi pulled up outside a terrace house with a green iron fence and a big brown door with a huge round handle in its middle. Mrs Reynold checked the sky, "Well, here we are. And just in time."

The street was wide. Not as wide as Victoria Parade, and not as busy, but it had tall trees running along it. They weren't elms, but they were just as pretty.

The second storey didn't have a balcony, it had two windows that looked out into the street and down at Coral. Little dots of cool water landed on her face, and she just knew it would be warm inside.

"Quickly, now." Mrs Reynold said, "It's about to pour down." She paid the driver and led Coral through the gate and inside the door.

"You can hang your coat here." Mrs Reynold placed her coat on the rack near the front door. There was a big man's grey coat and a smaller lady's coat already on the stand.

In the lounge room, a big girl with dark wavy hair waited for them. She shuffled to the edge of her seat on the couch. "Hello, Coral. My name is Violet. I'm sure we'll be firm friends."

Coral hid herself behind Mrs. Reynold's skirt while Violet continued. "I'm 15, how old are you?"

Violet didn't sound like one of those big mean girls at the Depot, and her smile looked friendly, instead of tricky. Coral crept from her hiding place. "Nine," she said, stretched her back tall and corrected herself, "Nine and a half."

"Nine and a half? My, that's very nearly ten." Violet patted the seat beside her on the floral couch. "Come sit with me."

Mrs Reynold removed her soft gloves and crossed the living room. "Yes, and I'll make some tea. Oh Arthur, come and meet Coral," she called and disappeared into the kitchen.

A grown man entered the lounge from the hallway. "Hmm Coral, you say?" he had a funny voice. Surely, he didn't talk like that all the time. Coral's eyes bugged open when he started stretching his braces in and out of his chest. Violet looked like she was trying not to laugh. What a funny man!

"No playing in the street. We've a yard for that." Mr Reynold gave his first command, complete with a wagging finger. "We don't want you all squished by a tram now, do we?"

Violet laughed, so Coral did too. Miss Griggs was right. Their home was so much nicer than the Depot.

Mrs Reynold, Violet, and Coral, stood around the kitchen table, with a very satisfied Mr Reynold patting his belly.

"What's the verdict, then?" Violet asked. "Whose biscuits[1] were the yummiest?"

"Oh, they were all delicious, of course. But the winner is... Coral, because I liked all the funny shapes she made with hers. Who needs boring old round biscuits, hey Coral?" Coral's smile spread warmth across her cheeks and into her throat.

"Bedtime now girls, off you go."

Coral followed Violet up the stairs to her very own room. It was small but was the first one she'd ever had to herself. It had floral wallpaper, a

---

1. Cookies

dresser, and a desk. She was sure it was the most beautiful bedroom in the whole world.

"I'm just next door," Violet said. Her bedroom was bigger and writing papers covered her desk. "Don't mind the mess," she said. "I'm going to be an editor when I grow up, so I must start practicing now. That reminds me..." With that, she began twirling and dancing on her toes. "I have to practice my ballet too."

Coral didn't know what an editor was, not that it mattered, but Violet's dance and the way she pointed her feet transfixed her.

"Come now, you two, time for bed." Mrs Reynold kissed Violet goodnight and led Coral back to her room. "Everything alright?" she asked.

Coral nodded and climbed into the soft bed.

"There are more blankets in the cupboard if you need them."

More blankets if I'm cold?

Mrs Reynold tucked her in and kissed her forehead. "Goodnight Coral, don't forget to say your prayers."

"I won't."

"Tomorrow we'll spend the day getting to know each other better. Then on Monday morning, we'll go into the city to get your new school uniform. Will that be alright with you?"

Coral nodded. "Will we go by tram?"

"Why, yes, we will."

"I like trams."

"So do I. Goodnight, dear."

"Goodnight."

Monday 20th May, 1940—Rathdowne St, Carlton

"Weetbix or eggs Coral?"

"Weetbix please."

Mr Reynold playfully grabbed at the newspaper Violet was reading. "My turn to read the paper, your turn to get ready for school, Violet."

"But look, look here, it's my poem."

"They've printed another? The Age had better pay you a salary. Alright, read it out to us."

"It's called *The Reason Why*," she said and stood at the head of the table.

'How strange, puffed Mr. Doubleday.
My trumpet simply will not play.
Isn't it strange said Tommy Tit?
Last night I laid an egg in it!'"

Coral laughed the loudest. How exciting to know someone who wrote something in the paper. She loved the way Violet had done her hair that morning, too. Violet made Coral want to smile and sigh all day.

Mrs Reynold walked faster than Coral, but not so fast she couldn't keep up. Her lovely gloves waved most of the way as she said 'good morning' or 'hello' to most people they met along the street. There was less fighting here, less angry words and shouting than at the boarding house. All the gardens were neat and tidy, and she especially loved the terrace houses that grew plants all up the side, and the houses with balconies with flowers trailing down from them. Everything seemed quieter ... quieter and slower. Ah! The boys weren't around making a ruckus. Coral smiled, funny how you can miss something annoying. The noise from all the kids in the Depot must've made up for it, but now she could hear the quiet, and the birds. Dad would like this street. Coral beamed when she thought of their reunion, and how excited she'd be to show him her new room.

Mrs Reynold took Coral's hand. "We're taking a different tram than we normally would. Can you keep a secret?" Coral nodded. Secrets were always fun.

"While we're in the city, we'll stop and collect the ballet shoes I ordered for Violet's birthday."

Coral's mouth hung open. Ballet shoes! She'd never even seen real ballet shoes before.

'Ding! Ding!' The tram ride wasn't as fun as Dad's. Mrs Reynold made Coral cross her ankles and sit with a straight back. 'Like a lady' she said. Most of the children she saw were on their way to school. Coral watched the colours of their uniforms and blazers change the further they travelled from Carlton. Soon there were no kids on the footpaths, just lots of men in hats and coats who looked very important and women with prams and paper parcels.

The city noise softened behind the door of the dance shop. Coral gaped at the leotards, tutus, and shoes with pieces of metal under them, but the satin ballet shoes in the display cabinet were extraordinary, with their wide ribbons draped around them like silky waterfalls.

The lady behind the counter wrapped Mrs Reynold's parcel with brown paper and tied it with string. Coral bounced on her tiptoes. Imagine how excited Violet will be!

The bell above the door rang while Mrs Reynold held it open. "Come now, this way," and as they stepped on to Elizabeth Street, a gust of wind made Mrs Reynold latch on to her hat.

"What a funny day, Coral. It's not cold, but the wind makes me worry for my hat!" she laughed.

Coral had never heard anyone laugh about the wind before. But she'd never met anyone like Mrs Reynold before, either.

In just a few blocks, they were at Flinders Street.

"A few more blocks this way," Mrs Reynold said as they rounded the corner, "Bell & Welch have uniforms on sale this week. That's very fortunate."

BANG!

Coral jumped back from the curb into Mrs Reynold's arms. A green car had crashed right into the back of the cream one. The drivers leapt from their cars and started arguing in the middle of the street. More men gathered around them as Mrs Reynold ushered Coral further up the street. It was a fright, but Coral was fascinated how the green car left its colour on the cream one, like a stripe. How funny if her uniform braid turned out to be green and cream!

Monday 20th May, 1940—Children's Welfare Department, Flinders Street Railway Building

Mrs Dulcie Shaw rode the elevator to the second floor of the Flinders Street Railway Building, straightening her skirt and tidying her curled dark hair. She collected the mail on the way past the reception desk. "Thank you, Janet," she called to the girl behind the desk, "Good morning."

"Good morning, Mrs Shaw," Janet called after her.

Dulcie's finger had half the envelope seal opened by the time she reached her office. A commotion in the street below led her to the large arched windows that overlooked the busy intersection. Another kerfuffle among motor car owners. Green and cream this time. Wonder what it is about that corner?

The envelope contained a note from the society of Prevention of Cruelty to Children and a cheque for 1 pound, 14 shillings, and 9 pence[2], towards the care of the Maxwell children.

Her colleague and office mate, John Oxford, passed the open door. "Oh, Mr Oxford..."

---

2. The pound £, was the currency of Australia from 1910 until 14 February 1966, when it was replaced by the Australian dollar. Like other £sd currencies, it was subdivided into 20 shillings (denoted by the symbol s or /–), each of 12 pence (denoted by the symbol d). To avoid confusion, I have spelt the currency throughout the book.

He back stepped into her view and pushed his dark-rimmed glasses to his face.

"Do you remember Mr Maxwell?" Mrs Shaw continued, "Placed his children into care about two months ago?"

"I think so. Wasn't it... Coral, Allan, and little....?"

"Ronald."

"That's them. Have you heard from him lately? He's meant to be making payments, but nothing's appeared yet."

"I'll see if the secretary's office has heard anything. Mrs Dawson should know."

"Righto."

Friday 24th May, 1940—
Mrs Snelling's Boarding House, Fitzroy

Albert Maxwell left his sandwich on the kitchen table and answered the ringing phone. "Yes, speaking. Oh, I see. I know I said I'd pay, it's just... You see, Mrs Dawson, it's the relief work. If there's none available, I'm just not getting work..."

He pulled the phone base closer to his chest and swapped the earpiece to the other ear.

"I understand Mrs Dawson really, I do... Yes, as soon as it comes to hand, I'll be sending it straight through.... Thank you, Mrs Dawson. Yes, nice talking to you too."

In the kitchen, Mrs Snelling's Polish sister-in-law looked up from shelling the peas. "Bad news?"

"For some. I need to get some money. Some work, Anna."

Anna closed her eyes so he wouldn't see her roll her eyes. Her sister-in-law said to be patient with the family man, but she felt she supported him, more than he supported her.

"Don't be like that, Anna. I'm serious, this is it."

"You've been serious before, remember, and it's come to naught."

"Give me a month. If I don't have work by then, I'll be out of your hair for good."

"Tramping?"

"No, I'll join up."

"You, in the army? That's one way to get everyone off your back, I suppose."

"Too right it will."

"Oooh! Wait till I tell Delia," she giggled.

"At least *she'll* be proud of me."

"I'm sure she will be, Mr Maxwell."

Thursday 6th June, 1940—Rathdowne St, Carlton

Mrs Reynold called up the stairway. "You'll be late girls, hurry up."
Violet and Coral giggled as they ran downstairs. They always seemed to run late.
"It's because I have to write in the morning, Mum... and Coral... Coral just takes all the time in the world to get ready!" The girls giggled again, grabbed their paper wrapped lunch and headed out the door.

Violet always walked Coral to her school and then went on to her own. They both wore dark blue tunics, but Violet had a special jacket called a blazer, and she had a hat too. It had a grey and gold band around it. Coral couldn't remember why she wanted it to be green and cream anymore, and she liked the grey and gold, anyway.
"Wish I got to wear a hat, too."
"You'd just lose it, silly. Besides, once you start wearing a hat, you can't do all that fun stuff like run around all day."
"I suppose."
"Still enjoying school?"
"We've got a spelling bee today."
"You're an excellent speller, Coral. You'll do well."
"Excellent. E-X-C-E-L-L-E... N-T. Excellent."
"See, you've got it in the bag."
Warmth spread in Coral's tummy and made its way to her cheeks, just like it often did when she was with Violet. She always made the half-hour

walk to school fun, and even told ghost stories about the scary ramshackle house on the corner. Her stories felt so real, Coral was glad she never passed it alone.

Violet waved goodbye at the school gate, and Coral saved her biggest wave for Mr Speight as he crossed the schoolgrounds. Coral always felt lighter around him and he was a fun teacher, except when he smacked her hands with his ruler when she wrote with her left hand. She practiced and practiced to please him. She heard people say he was eccentric, but Coral didn't really care about anyone's religion, anyway.

Mr Speight banned talk of the war in the classroom, and amongst the sea of navy uniforms and boring teacher's suits, he always wore some kind of bright colour. One time he was all in grey and the students wondered if he was ill, but at the end of the day, he put his feet on his desk and showed them he wore mustard socks! Coral never joined in when the boys played tricks on him, either. She was the most pleased when he smiled and said she'd done a good job.

Coral's stomach grumbled; the smells of tea cooking were irresistible.

"Can I set the table now?"

"Go on then Coral. Tea's not quite ready yet, but you may as well be doing something than standing around salivating."

"What's salivating?"

"Being very hungry."

It turned out it wasn't actually *years* before she ate, but only a short while later.

Violet gathered everyone's plates. "I'll do the washing up, Mum. Coral can dry."

"Before you do," Mrs Reynold said, "There's something I wanted to show you all. Look at this. Coral won her spelling bee!" She held up the certificate Coral had shown her when she got home from school. Heat flushed into Coral's cheeks but there was a delicious sensation in her tummy when they cheered and clapped for her.

"See, I told you you could do it!" Violet said.

Mrs Reynold stood. "We should celebrate… there's some fruit cake in the larder, and I'll heat some custard on the stove. Oh, and this came in the post today too," she handed a small package to Violet, who undid it carefully, making sure she didn't rip the stamps.

Something wrapped in tissue paper was inside, and Violet read the small note included with it.

"Oh, it's a prize from Ralph Rover from The Age!" She quickly unwrapped the tissue and discovered a photo album, filled with black paper and a packet of little corners to mark places to put the photos, so they all stayed in the right place. The outside was blue and after she'd looked at it, she let Coral look at all the special pages even though there were no photos in it yet.

After her bath, Coral joined Violet in the lounge room and they both snuggled in their pyjamas and read on the couch. Mr and Mrs Reynold spoke in low tones, or perhaps they were talking normally, but Coral was so engrossed in her book she didn't notice. She heard Mr Reynold say *'Dunkirk'* and it reminded her of how many times she'd heard that word recently and how the teachers and other grown-ups all wore soft frowns. Like frowns that weren't really there, but you knew they were underneath. All the grownups seem to tut and look quite sad. Coral put her book on her lap. "What's Dunkirk?"[3]

---

3. On May 10, 1940, Germany invaded France, pushing the British, French and Belgian Troops back towards the French port of Dunkirk. Operation 'Dynamo' was organised by the British Royal Navy to get the soldiers off the beaches and back to Britain. 338,000 soldiers were rescued by over 800 vessels including small vessels own by private citizens that made it across the English Channel and back with as many soldiers as they could carry.

"Nothing for you to worry about, little one." Mr Reynold came and sat in the lounge room with his pipe.

It was quiet for a little while. Then Mrs Reynold spoke, "I've got an idea. If the weather is fine, why don't we take the camera to the park on Saturday? We could have a picnic and take photos to put in Violet's new album."

"That's a marvellous idea, love." Mr Reynold said.

And just like that, Coral forgot all about whatever *Dunkirk* was, or wasn't, and looked forward to the weekend, making sure she crossed her fingers tight for fine weather.

Friday 21st June, 1940—Melbourne Town Hall

Bert shoved his hands deep into his coat pockets and concentrated on keeping his cigarette perched on his lips. The men who formed the line that ran along Swanston Street and into the Melbourne Town Hall appeared as cardboard cut-outs of each other. Coats fended off the cold, and puffs of rich tobacco contrasted against the dark grey of the footpath that couldn't dry in the intermittent rain.

The man in front leant back to Bert. "Hey mate. Good thing we weren't here yesterday, hey? It was pissing down!"[4]

"And so goddamn windy it woulda blown us back to Bourke Street!"

The men chuckled at their fortune and continued their banter through the Entrance Hall.

Around an hour later, Bert stood in front of a temporary desk. A bespectacled man in uniform asked him tired questions without looking up at his face.

"Name?"
"Albert Francis Maxwell."
"Date of Birth?"
"21st October, 1904."
"Address?"
"Southampton Street, Footscray."

---

4. Raining heavily

Thump! The rubber stamp sounded louder than he thought it would and left a mark across the man's papers. *Fit for Military Service.*

His friend from the queue grabbed his shoulders, "Me too! Young and Jackson's[5] to celebrate?"

"You betcha mate."

---

5. A popular Melbourne hotel

Friday 12th July, 1940—
C.W.D. Flinders Street Railway Building

Mr Oxford pushed the thick-rimmed glasses back onto his nose and dropped the notification letter onto his desk. "Well, it seems Maxwell has joined the Australian Imperial Forces, on the 1st of July, in fact."

Mrs Shaw stopped mid-type and considered the information. "Good on him. It should be good for him and his children. His payments will come through the military, and he won't be short of work, will he?"

"It seems they'll need all the help they can get. Did you see the paper this morning? Those Japanese look unpredictable, don't they?"

"Seems that way."

Mr Oxford shook the letter straight again. "Appears he's just been transferred to the 6th Training Battalion."

"Down at Mt. Martha?"

He nodded. "Look, it says a chap called Captain Henderson made an allotment of 1 shilling and 6 pence per week for each child to send to our office, but the military refused it as insufficient. New payments are suggested as 3 shillings for his wife and 3 shillings for children."

"But his wife left him."

"I suppose according to the army, he still legally has one."

Mrs Shaw shrugged and returned to her work. "Will they tell us if Mr Maxwell agrees to the new payment suggestion?"

"I don't know. But it'd be helpful to know wouldn't it?"

Saturday 21st September, 1940—
Australian Imperial Force Training, Darley

"Crikey Bert! Where 'ave you been?" a digger[6] shouted.

Albert staggered into the barracks; a metal shed built over concrete that housed part of the 2/8 Training Battalion. "Darley is the arse end of the world. I don't care who tries to correct me."

"Maxwell!" Albert was sick of the corporal's voice already, and he'd only just collapsed onto his straw mattress. "Get your arse to the C. O. now!"

The Commanding Officer was just about as happy as his corporal. "Private Maxwell. You were here for one week of your training. Then you chose to be Absent Without Leave for eight days. You've been *away* more than you've been here, private. This doesn't do well for morale, young man."

"No, Sir it doesn't."

"Six days confined to barracks."

"Yes, Sir."

---

6. Australian soldier

Wednesday 2nd October, 1940—
C.W.D. Flinders Street Railway Building

Mrs Shaw collected the mail from Janet and enjoyed a moment of their usual morning banter. "Oh, and Mrs Shaw, there's a call for you, I've just put it through."

Dulcie Shaw nodded and hurried to her office.

She arrived a little out of breath and lifted the receiver. "Hello, this is Mrs Shaw."

"Mrs Shaw. This is Albert Maxwell."

"Ah yes, Mr Maxwell, I've been expecting your call."

"Now, there seemed to be a bit of a to-do about my calling on Coral. I called ahead like you asked, and Mr Oxford said it would be fine, and yet when I got there, Mrs Reynold wouldn't let me take Coral for the weekend."

"Mr Maxwell, you understand that Mrs Reynold takes her position of Coral's guardian very seriously. She has spoken to us, and found that she couldn't, in all good conscience, grant your request to take Coral to unknown whereabouts for the weekend. She knows nothing about you and was concerned for her safety."

"But I'm her father."

"I understand, Mr Maxwell, but the stability of the children is what's most important right now, wouldn't you agree?"

"Yes, but—"

"Mrs Reynold cares sincerely about your family, Mr Maxwell."

"Listen, I have a friend that can take them, boarding out, just like Mrs Reynold does."

"We can look into that for you, Mr Maxwell, just have your friend complete the forms to confirm that their home is suitable. In the meantime, I'd like you to know Mrs Reynold has offered to take the other children as well, so they can be together, if that will ease your mind?"

"Of course it would. That'd be beaut, Mrs Shaw."

"So you'd agree to that situation if we can arrange it?"

"Definitely."

"Then leave it with me and I'll see what we can do. Thank you, and goodbye Mr Maxwell."

"Goodbye Mrs Shaw."

Mrs Shaw hastily scribbled a note on her desk pad. *Find Allan and Ronald Maxwell.*

First, it was the depression, then the war. Children came in faster than they could find homes for them. Even the beds at the Mental Hospital were being used. Women's Auxiliaries raised money for extensions and more beds, but it never seemed to be enough. Finding homes to board the children out to had become difficult too. The war and all its uncertainty caused people to pull their purse strings tighter; and the hesitancy was showing in the most practical of ways.

Saturday 5th October, 1940—Rathdowne St, Carlton

Mrs Reynold often had cups of tea with her neighbour, Mrs Watson. Mrs Watson had wrinkles and smelt like she'd splashed too much lavender water on her clothes, but she had the prettiest garden in the street. Coral could see Mrs Watson's backyard from her bedroom window, and watched all the colours of her flowers change as they grew. Mrs Watson often had her breakfast in the sun there, and she read the paper and sipped her tea and then just wandered the lawn of her garden looking at the garden beds with her hands behind her back. Maybe she was playing inspections, like the boys did at school, only she was inspecting her flowers, not soldiers.

Mrs Reynold stood at the front door. "Coral, would you like to join me in Mrs Watson's garden?"

"Yes, please." Coral left her colouring-in right where it was on the lounge room floor and as soon as they were out the front gate, spotted the dandelion growing on the naturestrip. She pulled it from the base of the plane tree and gave it a hefty blow.

"What did you wish for? Oh no, don't tell me, it won't come true." Mrs Reynold took Coral's hand. "Now, we need to remember how special Mrs Watson's flowers are, don't we?"

Mrs Reynold and Mrs Watson drank their tea and Coral walked along the garden edge looking at all the flowers. Mrs Reynold had already warned her not to pick them, so she was sure to admire them from afar.

"Another little waif? I don't know how you do it." Mrs Watson patted her friend's arm.

"Coral's such a sweet little thing."

"They still pay you for this service?"

"Seven shillings per day. It helps a little, but we always consider them part of our family, anyway."

"Of course you do."

"Her father's in the Australian Imperial Forces and has made enquiries about me taking one of her brothers as well."

Coral stopped short where she stood. Excitement pulsed through her limbs and down to her fingers and toes. Did she hear right? The boys? Coming here? She knew better than to speak out of turn, but also thought she might explode with joy. She bit the inside of her cheek so there was absolutely no chance she could mess anything up.

Wednesday 9th October, 1940—
C.W.D. Flinders Street Railway Building

Mrs Shaw rested the earpiece back on the base of the phone. "That was Mrs Reynold in Carlton. Young Ronald Maxwell has settled in well, and apparently Coral can't keep her hands off him. She also said that she'd like us to contact Mr Maxwell and let him know she kept her word and has Ronald with her."

"Well, that's good timing. We have to contact him, anyway."

"We do?"

Mr Oxford pulled a sheet of paper with a *zhing* from his typewriter and read, "Dear Mr Maxwell, it's been 88 days since you've made any payments towards the upkeep of your children. Et cetera, et cetera."

Mrs Shaw sighed. "So do we give him the good news, or the bad news first?"

"I don't think it matters very much."

"I suppose not."

Wednesday 9th October, 1940—Rathdowne St, Carlton

"Ronald, this is the kitchen, and this is living room," Coral held Ronald's hand and tore around the house showing him everything, "and these are Mrs Reynold's special teacups, you must never touch them, alright?"

Ronald managed half a nod before she jerked into the bathroom with stern instructions about bath time at the Reynold's household.

"And this is Violet, Ronald. She's very kind and lovely and she's got her sub-editor certificate from Ralph Rover of the Age. Do you know what that is? I'll tell you later and—"

Mrs Reynold appeared in front of them. "Whoa! That's a lot of energy you two have. How about we go for a walk instead?"

"To the park?"

"If you like."

Mrs Reynold had hardly closed the front gate behind them before Coral started again.

"This is Mrs Watson's house. She has the loveliest garden. If you're good, she lets you play in it sometimes."

And so it continued all the way to the park and all the way home again.

"Time for tea, and then a bath," Mrs Reynold said. "You must be exhausted. Coral, I'll set up a bed for Ronald in your room. Will that be alright?"

"Yes, please."

Mrs Reynold watched them say their prayers and tucked them both into bed and wished them a good night before she left the room.

Ronald turned over in his bed, "I like how your room isn't very dark."

"It's the streetlights."

Ronald tossed and turned, and harrumphed, and sighed.

"Come on then," Coral lifted her blanket for him. Ronald cuddled up nice and close, but it wasn't like it was before. Ronald was bigger, they didn't quite fit like they used to in Dad's bed, and he smelt different too. Still, she was sure his smile was as big as hers.

Tuesday 22nd October, 1940—
C.W.D. Flinders Street Railway Building

Mr Oxford tapped his pen on the desk and rolled his eyes. He leant his elbow on the desk, holding the earpiece and speaking into the tilted base of the phone. "Mr Maxwell, as we explained to you the last two times you have called, we would be derelict of our duties to let Coral just go with someone else willy-nilly. We have a duty of care that we take seriously."

"But this person is a friend of mine, a relative, in fact."

"And we will consider any appointment that your friend would like to make with us, that we might confirm their credentials. Have them complete the forms and bring them to the office. In the meantime, you agree that the children have a suitable home with Mrs Reynold, and it's best to avoid their disruption?"

"They're in good hands with Mrs Reynold, that's for sure, but I'll go and see my friend and call you about the appointment time."

"Certainly, Mr Maxwell. We'll wait for your call."

From her desk across the room, Mrs Shaw shook her head. "I wonder why his friend won't call or fill out the papers?"

"My dear Mrs Shaw, I wonder if we'll ever know."

1940—1942—2/8 Battalion A.I.F.

Bert Maxwell groaned in the throes of a savage hangover. A sturdy kick to his boot jarred through his spine and channelled straight into his painful head. His unfocused eyes opened to a familiar form. The corporal.

"Birthday celebrations was it, Maxwell? Back on base for two weeks, and then you're off again, Absent Without Leave for another 3 days!"

Bert groaned.

"C.O. now! Even if you have to crawl there!" The corporal rough handled him to headquarters and stood him in front of the Commanding Officer. The boot thump at the corporal's completion of 'atten-hut!', rattled inside Bert's brain.

"Look Maxwell, get yourself together, man! The Australian Army won't tolerate this behaviour from its men. Are you with us or not?"

"Don't suppose I have a choice, do I?" In a moment of clarity, he wondered if he'd spoken the words aloud, but no one arrested him, so he must've just thought it.

"Five days confined to barracks and a 5 pound fine."

Bert wobbled on his 'about face' but didn't really care.

The Corporal shook his head and mumbled as Bert left the room. "Happy birthday idiot."

Wednesday 9th April, 1941—Sydney Harbour

The 2/8 Battalion walked the gangplank to the largest ship Bert had seen in his life. "Here we go, lads."

"Jeez, those last six months were tough, eh?"

"And here we are on our way to the fighting." Bert checked the height from the gangplank to the water.

A soldier snorted. "Thought you wouldn't make it this far."

"What? I was only in the hospital for five days."

"How's that though, gettin' a break from training for your wisdom teeth?"

Another chimed in, "At least we know you're a bleeder now, not once we're out there."

Bert stopped and pointed his finger at them. "Bleeder my arse. It was that bloody dentist, didn't do his job properly. Despite that, those nurses at Sale made a delightful change from your ugly mugs[7]."

"If you weren't going to bleed to death, I thought they'd throw you for all your AWLs."

"There weren't too many…"

"There were enough, mate. How many fines and days' pay? How many 'confined to barracks'?"

Bert wiped at his chin. "Meh, lost count. Still here with you now, aren't I boys? And on the *Queen Mary* no less."

Tuesday 10th June, 1941—2/8 Battalion, Gaza Ridge, Palestine

The diggers of the 2/8 Battalion lay around inside large canvas tents and sweated in the Middle Eastern heat.

"So, this is Palestine, hey?"

"Day after day of sand and heat."

"Just think of it as a stinking hot day at St Kilda beach."

---

7. Faces

"... yeah, but with no water."
"... and no sheilas[8]."
"... sand as far as the eyes can see."
"... and no cool change."
"What I'd do to feel a breeze gliding across the bay."

There was nothing to do but wait.
And dig latrines, train, have a game of cricket, and wait.... and sweat.

Thursday 31st July, 1941—
2/2nd Australian General Hospital,
El Kantana Suez Canal, Egypt

Bert Maxwell sauntered into the medical tent at Gaza Ridge. "God doc, can't believe this hurts so much."

"What now Maxwell?"

Bert undid his shirt and lifted his arm to reveal a tender reddish lump in his armpit.

"Hmm," the doctor gently palpated the mass.

"Ow! Fuck, watch it!"

"Well, it happens in the desert, in this heat. It's too infected to deal with here." The doctor pulled out some papers. "We'll send you to the 2nd Australian General Hospital. There's a truck headed to El Kantara this afternoon. I'll organise your paperwork with the Commanding Officer. Be on it."

The hospital was no more than hospital beds inside canvas tents but still better than sleeping on the floor.

"Abscess of Axilla, what does that mean Doc? Is it bad?"

"What it means, Private Maxwell, is that you've developed an abscess under your arm. Most likely through a hair follicle. That's why your arm is

---

8. Women

so painful to move and heavy. We'll treat the infection here and get you well and back to your unit as soon as possible. Rest here a while and recover."

"Oh, righto then Doc," Bert propped his arms above his head on the surrounding pillows "I can do that. Thanks, mate."

<u>Saturday 20th September, 1941—</u> ### *<u>2/8 Battalion Gaza Ridge, Palestine</u>*

Another hot and windy day blasted sand in and around the medical tent. A gust of warm air flicked the pages of the doctor's never-ending paperwork and announced the entry of another patient, standing to attention and awaiting his services.

"You arrived back from 2nd AGH yesterday, didn't you Maxwell?"

"Yes, Sir."

"And here you are in my tent again, seeking medical attention?"

"Yes, Sir."

"What is it this time?"

"My ankle, Sir."

"Stand easy, let me see. ... it looks like more infected follicles."

"Seems that way, Sir."

"Hmph. The last thing we need here is a staph outbreak. Off to the 2nd AGH again, I'll find out when the next truck is leaving."

"Well, only if you say so, Doc."

Thursday 5th February, 1942

Albert Maxwell embarked the S.S. Strathallan hospital ship bound for Australia.

<u>Friday 20th February, 1942—Rathdowne Street, Carlton</u>

"Oh, that's horrible news, what will we do?"

"Don't fuss Violet, not in front of the littlies," Mrs Reynold said and continued preparing their breakfast.

"But it's becoming so real, isn't it? So close."

Violet plonked the newspaper down on the kitchen table.

Air Raids on Darwin![9] Coral couldn't miss seeing the bold headline.

She didn't know where Darwin was, but knew it was in Australia somewhere. "They were bombed?"

"Yes, but... the reason you shouldn't worry is..." Mrs Reynold's voice trailed off, and she frowned at Violet.

Violet patted Coral's arm. "Remember last week how we stood out the front and watched all the houses put cardboard up in their windows, and all the streetlights dimmed?"

Coral nodded. "And the cars had those funny black caps on their headlights?"

---

9. The Bombing of Darwin, also known as the Battle of Darwin, on 19 February 1942 was the largest single attack ever mounted by a foreign power on Australia. On that day, 242 Japanese aircraft, in two separate raids, attacked the town, ships in Darwin Harbour and the town's two airfields in an attempt to prevent the Allies from using them as bases to contest the invasion of Timor and Java during World War II.

"That's it. Do you remember what it was called?"

"Brown out."

"That's right."

"Did you remember what Mr Reynold told you the *black*out was for?"

"Everything turns off. Even the trams stop so the planes with bombs can't see us."

"That's right."

"So, did the Darwin people leave their lights on?"

"Umm, not quite. But anyway, we are very, very far away from Darwin, aren't we Mum?"

"Yes, that's so right. You could even ask Mr Speight today at school. I bet he can tell you how many miles exactly."

"I would love to know the answer, too."

"Do you think you could remember it and tell us all at teatime tonight?"

Coral nodded. It didn't matter about the bombs anymore; she was on her own mission.

Monday 16th March, 1942

Albert Maxwell disembarked the S.S. Strathallan hospital ship in Adelaide.

Monday 27th April, 1942—
2/2nd AGH, Watten Siding, Hughenden, Queensland

The Commanding Officer paced his office. Every available hand was needed now the 2nd AGH had arrived at Hughenden and begun the task of reinstalling itself on new ground. With increased fighting in the Pacific, it was vital to have a hospital close to the action; one that was operating and fully equipped as soon as possible.

"Have you found Maxwell yet? Where the bloody hell is he, Staff Sergeant?"

"He's taken off again. Apparently soon after we docked in Adelaide."

"Alright, take this down then. AWL. Failing to appear at the place of parade. Fined four days' pay."

"Thank God, they assigned him to us. What would have happened if he'd pulled this stunt on the field? Would you want him backing you up?"

"Can't say I would, Sir. But how are we going to fine him if we can't find him?"

"We'll have to send it off to the Court of Inquiry, he's left us no choice."

Friday 22nd May, 1942—Court of Inquiry, Canberra

Illegal absence—Court of Inquiry

Court of Inquiry held at Canberra declared that Pte Maxwell AF illegally absented himself without leave from 2/2nd Aust Gen Hosp AIF on 1st April 1942, and that he is still so absent and that on the 22nd May 1942 he was deficient, and that he is still deficient of articles to the value of 17 pound, 5 shillings, and 10 pence.

<u>Sunday 24th May, 1942—Rathdowne St, Carlton</u>

The morning sun streamed through Coral's bedroom. It was already cold enough to wear jumpers to school, so a sunny day was most welcome. Perfect for afternoon tea at Cynthia's house after school. A wonderful birthday tea with cordial and cake with some of the other girls from school. Mrs Reynold bought a pretty ribbon as a gift, and Coral had wrapped it herself. The paper was a bit crinkled, and it was hard to get the string just right, but Coral couldn't wait to give it to Cynthia and see how pretty it looked in her hair. She made sure the gift was safe on the dresser and turned to Ronald as he rubbed his eyes.

"Time to get up, sleepyhead. I'm going to Cynthia's after school. I can't wait."

A thump and a scream shot its way up the staircase, and Coral drew Ronald into a tight squeeze.

It was Mrs Reynold. "Arthur!" she cried. "Arthur! Violet! Oh Arthur! Violet!"

Violet's footsteps thumped on the stairs, then stopped halfway and came back to their room. Her face looked very pale, like the time she was sick in bed.

"You two stay here. I'll be back soon." and she pulled the door closed.

Coral nodded and waited quietly but couldn't hear what the crying and muffled urgent talking was about.

She busied herself, got Ronald dressed, read him a book, and played some games, and pretended not to hear the intermittent wailing, the 'oh no's' and the soothing words coming from downstairs. A car pulled up outside, and the doctor who came to see Violet, lifted his hat, and walked through the gate. Mrs Watson led him inside. She usually breakfasted outside in her garden on sunny days, then she'd wander the garden sipping her tea. Her newspaper flapped in the breeze on her patio table, and her tea looked still and cold. She'd never left her garden before. More mumbles travelled up the stairs, but Coral couldn't make anything of it.

Coral's stomach rolled. Something was wrong. Horribly wrong, and she shut her eyes tight and opened them again. Maybe if she stayed in her room long enough, pointing out the dust in the rays of sunlight to Ronald, and being the *goodest girl* she could be, whatever was happening *down there* might not make its way up the stairs to her. Then she could continue being happy about the sunny day today, and the crinkled gift paper on the dresser.

There was a tap at the door, and Mrs Watson's face appeared around it. "Come now, children, gather your things." Her lips were pinched, and she had wet eyes. "Let me escort you to school today. Let's go through the side garden into mine."

"I'm hungry" Ronald said.

"Well, I'll get your breakfast for you then."

Coral didn't want to ask Mrs Watson what was wrong. And she didn't feel much like breakfast, anyway. She placed the ribbon carefully into her school bag, laying it between two books to protect it.

Things were different after Mr Reynold died. As if all the happiness had been sucked out of the home and got run over on the busy road. Squished, just like he said to her when she first arrived. Mrs Reynold was always too tired to bake, or to listen to her read, or to even cook dinner.

"Not now dear," she'd say.

Violet took over a lot of the housework, and Coral helped as much as she could. But Violet didn't smile so much and stopped writing, too. Whenever Coral saw Violet at her desk, she was just staring out the window, not working, and without a pen in her hand at all.

Mrs Reynold was always asleep on the couch, or so tired she couldn't talk properly, and Violet would put her to bed. No one smiled very much; just those pretend ones you wear when you're meant to be brave.

Goodbye Carlton

Children's Welfare Department
Royal Park Receiving Depot, Parkville
19.07.1942

Maxwell, Coral 13.9.30
Admitted 19.07.1942 from Mrs Reynold, Carlton.

Condition—Appears healthy.
Particular marks on body—Scar on knee
Condition of clothing—Good

Additional Notes—Mrs Reynold drank and exploited the children.

Parkville II

1942

<u>*Sunday 19th July, 1942—Royal Park Depot, Parkville*</u>

The Depot looked different this time, and not just because both Coral and her surroundings were two years older. Perhaps she wasn't so shocked this time. She knew what to expect, and she knew the difference between a warm home, and nice clothes, and a good school, and feeling cared for, and... this.

"Come on, then Coral." A skinny little lady with spiky fingers dragged them through her hair.

"I don't have lice." But she knew her words were in vain; they'd still wash her hair with kero again.

"There's a scar on your knee."

Coral looked down at the little red mark. "That's where I tripped on the footpath and Violet put this stinging stuff on it. It hurt in the bath too, but Mrs Reynold said the best part was that it didn't get infected."

"True. That *is* the best part."

"She's very sad, you know... Mrs Reynold. Did you know Mr Reynold died?"

"I heard that. And it's in your notes. I'm sure Mrs Reynold is very sad."

Another thing that was different about the Depot this time, was that Mr Reynold didn't say he was coming back soon. Coral knew where she stood with him. Even if she stood all alone, at least she wasn't guessing anymore.

Mrs Reynold always made sure things were colourful, yet it was forever grey and dreary at the Depot. She hadn't noticed that before. Or the noise, so much noise; like everything clattered because there wasn't anything soft around to make it be quiet.

Miss Griggs wasn't there anymore, either. She probably went somewhere where Mrs Silcock couldn't yell at her for every little thing.

At least school was a bit better. Being nearly twelve made her one of the older girls there. But she missed Mr Speight and his coloured socks and vests and ties terribly.

Coral sighed a deep and heavy sigh.

Now to wait again, for someone *suitable*.

Wednesday 11th November, 1942—
C.W.D. Flinders Street Railway Buildings

Mr John Oxford pushed his dark-rimmed glasses back to the bridge on his nose, as was his way when opening envelopes. He leaned back in his office chair and called across the office to Mrs Shaw.

"The Victorian Society for the Prevention of Cruelty to Children are holding 2 pound, 4 shilling, and 4 pence of Albert Maxwell's relief work wages in the interest of his wife. They're saying they've now completely lost track of the Maxwells and are forwarding the money to the department as a contribution toward the children's care."

"Every little bit helps."

Mr Oxford stamped the letter as 'received' and added it to the Maxwell file. "That it does, Mrs Shaw."

Saturday 26th December, 1942—Ascot, Brisbane

"Maxwell, you're just not the full quid[1] are you? What did you think they'd do?" Bert's defence officer shook his head and paced the interview room in Ascot, Brisbane. He stopped briefly and checked on the two military police who guarded the door.

Bert slumped back in his seat, picking at his fingers. "Not bother lookin' for me after a while?"

The officer stopped and pulled documents from his briefcase. "You had a good trot[2], didn't you? Says here you lasted from the 1st April through to the 4th November, but you'd have to be thick as two short planks[3] to think they wouldn't find you. They suspended your payments too, you know that? Since the 1st of April."

"Well, it wasn't like I was about to collect them, was I?"

The defence officer slapped a file onto the empty table. "What about your kids?" He flipped some papers toward Bert. "And your wife?"

"God knows where she's got to. Old slag."

---

1. Not very bright

2. Good luck

3. Stupid

"They've got you on two counts, although they could've got you for more."

"You telling me to be grateful?"

"I'm telling you that the court of inquiry has already charged you, and now you've added to that... let me see, 1. Disobeying a lawful command given by his superior officer, and 2. Impeding the Provost Marshall in the execution of his duty."

"So?"

"Private Maxwell, when we walk in there, I advise you to take whatever they give you on the chin."

The two military police officers led Bert back into the sparse interview room. His defence officer followed a few minutes behind.

"That wasn't too bad, hey Maxwell? What I mean is, it could've been a lot worse."

"So you keep telling me."

"Look, you've already spent 51 days in detention, they've slapped you with another 28 days and a 5 pound fine."

Bert shrugged.

"After that, you'll be sent back to the 2/2nd Australian General Hospital where you're *supposed* to be, and where you'll *stay* until told otherwise. They're based somewhere up north now, Atherton I think. The Army has also reinstated your allotments payments to your children from 2nd January. You'll be glad to hear that."

"Yeah, righto."

LISA KING

<u>*Monday 22nd February, 1943—*</u>
<u>*2/2nd Australian General Hospital, Atherton, Queensland*</u>

The Secretary
Welfare Department
Railway Buildings
Flinders Street
Melbourne

Dear Sir,
Pte. Maxwell, who is attached to this unit has spoken to me of his concern for his children—Coral, Allan, and Ronald, two of whom are in the care of Mrs Reynold of Rathdowne St, Carlton.

He tells me that he saw the two in the charge of Mrs Reynold when on leave nearly 12 months ago, and that he was not allowed to take them out and always spoke to them in the presence of Mrs Reynold.

He has not had any news from them for some time and is naturally anxious and such anxiety gnaws at a man on active service and reacts in various ways on his life and work.

I should be very happy if you can help us in this matter,

Yours Sincerely,
Chaplain James Waterman

P.S. He tells me he is contributing 3 shillings and 6 pence a week from his pay towards their maintenance. Is this in addition to their allowances from the Army?

LISA KING

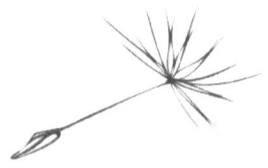

Monday 1st March, 1943—
C.W.D. Railways Buildings Flinders Street

Chaplain James Waterman
2/2nd A.G.H. (A.I.F)
Rocky Creek
Via Atherton
North Queensland

Dear Sir,
I have your letter of the 22nd ultimo and desire to inform you that the children are no longer with Mrs Reynold, as her domestic circumstances had altered.

Allan and Ronald are at Melrose Boy's Home, Berwick, about 25 miles from Melbourne and which is conducted by the Try Boys Society.

There are about 20 picked boys there who are under a very understanding superintendent and matron and could not be better cared for; some of the boys who have won scholarships attend Dandenong High School 5 miles away.

Coral is at Royal Park Children's Depot and is receiving good care.

DANDELION WISHES

This department receives Dependant's allowance of 10 shillings and sixpence per week, and military allotment of 3 shillings and sixpence per week for each of the 3 children, of which 9 shillings per week each is maintenance, and the balance is placed to the children's savings accounts.
Yours faithfully,
Secretary

Thursday 15th April, 1943—Royal Park Depot, Parkville

Coral waited longer this time. She watched kids come and go; some stayed alongside her, waiting for someone deemed suitable. Others were the right age for families who could afford to feed another mouth. She was at that other end. Definitely not cute like the babies, or strong like the boys.

Patience. That's what Mrs Reynold had called it. When you simply had to wait, when you didn't want to wait anymore. Coral tried hard but wasn't any good at it.

Beds, breakfast, dress, school, there never seemed to be anything of value going on. School wasn't fun anymore. Mr Marks yelled and threatened the cane all the time, and he used it. Coral was terrified; the most disobedient thing she did was close her eyes sometimes when she was meant to be working. She'd pretend she had magic powers and could see all the way to Princes Hill and could see what colour Mr Speight's socks were that day, or whether he wore a coloured tie.

The only thing better than last time, was that on Saturdays, Coral was one of the older girls. No more crawling around on her knees waxing the floor; she held the tin of polish like a trophy.

Coral stretched out on her bed and enjoyed her full tummy. Anne Whittaker didn't want to finish her stew, and she gave the rest to Coral. She ate it all up, even the chewy bits, and now she was deciding whether her tummy was, in fact, a bit too full.

Mrs Thompson walked past her bed. She was one of the nicer ladies. "Coral, you'll need to gather your things."

Coral scrambled from her bed and her daydreams of an exploding stomach. "Where am I going?"

"There's a place become available for you at the Catherine Booth Home."

"Who's Catherine Booth?[4] Is she nice?"

Mrs Thompson rolled her eyes. "Just do as you're told and get your things ready. Mrs Shaw will drive you there tomorrow."

"Alright."

There was no point asking questions. Excitement bubbled in Coral's tummy; thinking about her new home, but there was also a dragging sensation inside her, a fear of not knowing where she was going, and why.

Coral looked around, but she didn't have anything of her own to pack up, anyway.

---

4. Catherine Booth was co-founder of The Salvation Army, along with her husband William Booth. Because of her influence in the formation of The Salvation Army she was known as the 'Mother of The Salvation Army'. Many hospitals, family shelters and children's homes around the world carry her name.

Goodbye Parkville II

Children's Welfare Department

Secretary's Office
16.4.43

Received from the Secretary of the Children's Welfare Department, the child—female—named in the margin (MAXWELL, Coral 13.9.30), in good health being transferred to East Kew.

Signed,
B Bradbury.

East Kew

1943

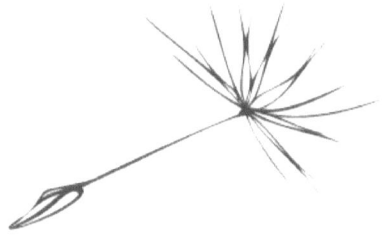

<u>Friday 16th April, 1943—</u>
<u>Catherine Booth Home for Girls, East Kew</u>

"I've had three homes, Mrs Shaw; my dad's, the Depot, Mrs Reynold's and now this."

Mrs Shaw nodded and manoeuvred the car around the curve of the circular driveway. Before them, a huge grey mansion rose from the grounds. Coral's mouth hung open. "Look at all the arches over the verandas. It makes it look like a castle! Am I going to live in a castle?"

Mrs Shaw held her hat against the windy day. "Come along Coral," and they crunched their way along the gravel driveway, past the tall palm tree, and to a solid green front door.

Mrs Shaw pushed the door open and Coral gaped at the polished staircase, polished floors and well-scrubbed landings. There were girls everywhere, wearing navy blue tunics, all on their way to somewhere as if they had something to do. Mrs Reynold used to call that being *purposeful*. The girls pushed past each other as they came down the staircase.

"New girl," some whispered to their companions, and Coral's tummy relaxed when many met her blank stare with a welcoming smile.

A lady approached them. She was wearing a uniform, but it wasn't a scary looking one. It was very dark blue, and her collar stuck straight up along her neck and had an '*S*' on it.

Mrs Shaw held out her hand. "Matron Bradbury, this is Coral Maxwell. Another girl for you, I'm afraid."

"No need to worry, Mrs Shaw. The Salvation Army will find some room. We always do." She smiled, and Coral's lips formed a wobbly smile in return.

Matron Bradbury motioned for Mrs Shaw to join her in the office and placed a hand on Coral's shoulder. "Off you go, Coral, go outside and play. Lunchtime play will be over soon enough. Just follow the other girls into school when you hear the bell."

Coral followed where the trail of girls had led earlier, listening as the sounds of play got louder the closer she moved to the back door.

Girls of all sizes and ages filled the yard. Some scrambled in and out of an old tram, others played on swings. There was so much noise, but it was a cheerful noise. Some younger girls were making pies in the sandpit. Ronald would have loved that sandpit; she'd be tempted to play herself only she was now twelve and a half, and a bit big for that sort of thing.

Coral's eyes widened at the sight of the in-ground pool. It was out of season now and draining, with dirt and leaves around the small puddle at the bottom. She hoped it wasn't broken and might learn to swim here. When the Reynolds went to the beach, she'd just played in the shallows.

Pine trees reached up to the sky, and she almost got knocked over by girls playing tiggy[1]. They used her as a barrier between them, giggling and dodging this way and that, and then ran off again.

Two older girls left their group and stepped toward her. Coral twisted her fingers in the belt of her light green dress as the navy-blue wall closed in on her. One girl was much bigger than Coral, she had a kind of frizzy light brown hair. The other girl, with dark straight hair like Violet's, was closer to Coral's size.

---

1. Tag, chasey.

"What's ya name?" the girl with the frizzy hair asked.

"Coral."

"Like that stuff in the ocean?"

"I suppose so."

"Hello Coral!" the dark-haired girl thrust her hand at her to shake. "Pleased to meet you."

Coral took her hand to shake as the big girl commented again.

"Oh Allison, how many times have I told you not to be so trusting? You've got to learn to be a bit suspicious, alright?"

"But Coral's trustworthy, isn't she? I mean, look at her."

"You never know; I've told you so many times. Be careful. People aren't always kind. Woulda thought you'd know this by now."

"I know you're right, Constance. I keep forgetting. Besides, Coral's a *kid*."

A bell sounded at the back of the yard near a small brick building. A girl stood in front of it swinging a brass bell with both hands.

"Come on Coral," Allison took her hand, "You can sit next to me."

The classroom was dark after the sunshine outside, but it was cosy enough with desks laid in rows. Allison led Coral to her desk and told her where to sit. "This is Coral. She's a new girl." She told anyone and everyone that walked past and took their seats.

Across the aisle from her, Constance talked to the girl beside her. She didn't seem so scary now she wasn't looming over her.

The click-clack of the teacher's shoes arrived in the classroom before her. "Quiet now girls."

Allison tugged on Coral's sleeve. "That's Mrs Paynter."

They worked hard on times tables and then had some free time for weaving. The girls were all weaving scarves for the soldiers. It was too late for Coral to start hers, but they were going to knit socks next, so she looked forward to that. She'd never seen anyone weave before and thought Allison was terribly clever.

Coral was starving by tea time. Her belly grumbled, so she didn't mind the rice at all.

"You'll soon get sick of it," Constance whispered as she pushed the rice around her plate.

Allison leaned forward. "And the sago[2]."

"Hush!" an officer said. "No talking in the dining room." It meant all they did was eat, and that suited Coral just fine.

"Quick! Toilet before it's dark!" Allison grabbed Coral's hand and flew down the stairs.

"Girls!" an officer barked. "Walk nicely, please. You're not animals!"

Coral pulled up the sides of her too-big nightdress. "What happens when it's dark?"

"It's scary down here, not that I would come at night, anyway. But it's best to empty yourself before bedtime."

Did Allison sometimes wet the bed too?

"Otherwise, you need to use the pail."

"The what?"

"The pail, silly. It's a bucket we use in the dorm, so we don't have to come out here at night. Don't worry," she added, "You'll get put on the roster to empty it like everyone else!"

Then she ran into the toilet, leaving Coral wondering how she'd carry the pail down all those stairs!

---

2. Sago is a starch extracted from the pith, or spongy core tissue, of various tropical palm stems and is similiar to tapioca, but sourced by a different method.

Most girls were in bed by the time they returned. Their room had lots of white steel beds, maybe ten or twenty; all lined up and not a wrinkle on the white bedspreads. Coral read the writing that was on each bedspread. *God. Is. Love.*

"Lights out, goodnight girls."

Coral tried hard to stay awake; to think about the day and say her prayers, but she was so exhausted she fell asleep straight away.

<u>Monday 14th June, 1943—
Catherine Booth Home for Girls, East Kew</u>

Coral's eyes shot open.

Oh no!

No! no! no! no! no!

The early morning light made the dorm look grey. She moved a little and confirmed her worst fears. She hadn't wet the bed for two months, and now this.

She knew her fate.

From now on, she'd have to sleep on the balcony. That's where all the bedwetters slept, rain, hail, or shine.

Of course, it was Adjutant Rutter who found out first.

"Why is your nightdress wet, Coral? Did you wet your bed?"

Coral wished she'd lower her voice. But Adjutant Rutter just kept on about it. There were nearly one hundred girls in the home now. And thanks to Rutter, she bet every one of them knew!

"Pure Laziness! That's all it is. We try hard to instill morals in you girls and look at how you repay us. Best get your bed out onto the balcony."

"But it's so cold out there."

"It's easy then, isn't it? Don't want to sleep on the balcony? Don't wet the bed! You'll make the rest of us smell. It really is a dirty thing to be doing, Coral."

The rest of the day ran like its regimented self.

Everyone was up at 6.30am for a quick wash. Coral moved her bed out to the balcony and rather than turn it like they did every morning, she tried her best to air it in the cold and damp June weather.

Being one of the older girls, she helped dress the little ones in the morning; cleaned their faces, made their beds, and got them ready for breakfast. It was like a production line, well that's what Constance said they were called. Where people worked in factories and did one job and passed the thing onto the next person until it was finished. She said it had to do with munitions and the war. The morning routine made her think of Ronald. Did he have someone to remind him to brush his teeth and wash behind his ears? She much preferred getting the little ones ready than the other morning chores of making beds, cleaning the kitchen, or sorting the laundry.

Then it was time to head downstairs for a breakfast of Weetbix or toast, and sweet tea, then on to school or the chores for the day. School, even when it was hard, was always better than doing chores.

Saturday morning started with a thick slice of bread and dripping, followed by a quarter cup dose of Epsom Salts. Then they had to wait in line for the toilet and hope that someone had cut enough squares of newspaper for them all.

Saturday was also hair washing day. Constance said it was sheep dip they washed in, to get rid of lice and fleas, but the officers told her to shut up, so Coral didn't know who to believe.

On the weekends, everyone helped with chores. There seemed to be a never-ending list of dusting, washing, and polishing floors, salting the cups, and scrubbing the quadrangle. At first, Coral loved polishing the beautiful balustrade. Soon she was sick of the sight of it! At the top of the stairs, on the outer wall of the corridor, there were three lead light windows of native birds. Coral would look at the birds and imagine they were cheering her on, *"Come on Coral, get the chores done and you can go and play."*

Once a fortnight on the weekend, families could visit. They'd bring picnics and have lunch on the lawn together. Coral would watch them from the balcony and wonder what the boys were up to. Did they find families to take care of them? She hoped they weren't sleeping outside on a cold balcony, too.

The girls ran to the roster board. Constance, as usual, got there first and slung her head back and groaned. "Ugh! In the laundry with Major Fishwick again."

Allison pushed her out of the way to read her assignment for the week. "Stop being cheeky, and they'll stop giving you the awful jobs, Constance. Besides, if you're in the laundry, you might get to talk to the boys."

"Oooh Carey Grammar boys." Coral laughed.

Constance laughed too. "Remember how worried that boy was when the bell rang and you wouldn't give him his hat back?"

"Hmm," Allison said, "I'd expect he'd get into a lot of trouble going back to class without his hat. Or for talking to girls and 'homies' at that!"

Constance nudged Coral as they all laughed. "I thought he was going to pee his pants!"

Allison nodded thoughtfully. "That'll teach him for kicking the ball down to our fence."

"Oh, Allison, you dill, they do it on purpose."

"Do they really?"

Coral and Constance nodded at her.

"Really?"

Constance rolled her eyes at her and did a silly walk toward the laundry.

Allison called after her, "Don't get your fingers caught in the mangler[3] again!"

Coral loved her turn in the scullery, preparing the vegetables for the following day. The only thing that put a dampener on it was that Adjutant Rutter was in charge of the kitchen, but the other officer there, Captain Tait, was always nice to be around. Coral would happily sit for hours shelling peas, peeling potatoes, and getting the kitchen ready for upcoming meals.

Adjutant Rutter strode into the scullery. "I'm after volunteers to pick some fruit. You two, Tania and Marjory; go and get some washing baskets." Tania and Marjory put their knives down and rolled their eyes while Adjutant Rutter continued. "Mrs Bentley, at number 49, has some oranges that she's kindly donated to us. Best behaviour now girls, off you go."

A whispered voice woke Coral up. "Hurry and get ready. I'll be waiting downstairs."
Coral rubbed at her eyes in the dark. "What time is it?"
"Two thirty."

---

3. Rollers used for squeezing excess water from washing.

The officer's silhouette stepped quietly through the rows of beds. It was early Thursday morning and Coral's turn to take the tram with Officer Chapman and another girl to the Victoria Market.

Once there, the girls followed Officer Chapman through the many rows of fruits and vegetables as she asked for donations for the home.

"What lovely apples you have today, Mr Parker."

Mr Parker lifted his hat. "Thank you, Mrs Chapman," he reached for a large crate behind him. "I've got these for your girls this week." The apples were funny shapes, and some had spots on them, but in Coral's eyes they were perfect. "Shall I drop them to the home for you on my way back?"

"That would be helpful, thank you."

Coral breathed a sigh of relief. When he'd brought out the crate, she'd wondered how they would ever get them on the tram!

The girls carried a sack each for the donations. Constance hated this job; she said it was like they were begging for food, but Coral didn't care how they got the fruit. Just that they got it. Coral's favourite part was when stall holders would give the girls a mandarin or a pear as a treat for the trip home.

"It's Sunday tomorrow girls," Constance was taking big important steps around the dorm pretending to be an officer. She spun around quickly and pointed at Susan. "Hush back there! No talking!" and all the girls laughed.

Every Sunday, every girl in the home attended the Salvation Army Citadel at Kew. They passed the half-hour walk in silence, just as Constance described. Coral thought conversation would make the time pass quickly, but the officers obviously didn't agree. Still, the walk was pleasant. The little ones went to Sunday School, while the bigger girls sat in church.

Then, they'd gather again for another silent half an hour's walk home.

LISA KING

<u>Monday 30th August, 1943—</u>
<u>2/2nd Australian General Hospital, North Queensland</u>

The Secretary
Children's Welfare Department
Melbourne

Dear Sir,
I am writing to you on behalf of Pte A.F. Maxwell of this unit.
In 1939, he committed his daughter Coral Maxwell to the care of the department.
She, on his return from the Middle East, was seen by him at Royal Park House, Royal Park, several times.
The father of Coral Maxwell cannot get his letters answered. He has had no reply to his letters to his daughter. And I have in my possession a letter of his addressed to Miss Coral Maxwell c/- Royal Park House, Royal Park, returned to him marked "Try Mental Hospital" and "Not known at Mental Hospital Royal Park".
Mr Maxwell is most anxious to know where his daughter is located and to why those in charge of Royal Park House do not give him her address.

The child is 13 years of age next month and is quite able to write to her father. If all is well with her, would you please see what can be done about tracing Coral Maxwell, and let me know.

Yours Sincerely,
WR Chaney
Chaplain 2/2nd Australian General Hospital

Wednesday 15th September, 1943—
C.W.D. Flinders Street Railway Building

Chaplain WR Chaney
2/2nd Australian General Hospital
North Queensland

Dear Sir,
Re- Coral Maxwell
With reference to your recent letter, I have to inform you that the above-named girl is at the Salvation Army Girl's Home, Sackville St, East Kew, to which letters may be addressed to her. I would state that girls at the abovenamed home are encouraged to write to their relatives.

Yours faithfully,
Secretary

Thursday 14th October, 1943—
Catherine Booth Home for Girls, East Kew

The air-raid siren blasted through the air and straight into Coral's eardrums like shattered glass. Her heart pounded, more from the horrible noise than all the shouts of "Quickly girls! Hurry Up!"

Little bodies in nightshirts scurried in the darkness; along the corridor, down the staircase, and around to the back of the home. Then down into the air raid trenches, where they waited wide eyed in the dark. Was it a drill... or real this time? Coral listened hard for the sound of aeroplanes but could only hear the panting breaths of her friends.

"Ugh," Constance complained. "Why'd they have to do it when it rained? My feet are muddy."

"Constance!" That was Adjutant Rutter. "Do you think the enemy will only bomb us in fine weather? No! We must prepare for all eventualities!"

Constance nudged Coral and whispered, "It's still bloody cold and miserable down here."

"I don't know how I'll ever get back to sleep," Coral said to the darkness and took Constance's hand, "Here, feel that! My heart's just about beating out of my chest."

"Parkdale." It was Allison's voice, somewhere in the dark.

"What?"

"Parkdale. I always think of Parkdale when I need to sleep."

"What's Parkdale?"

Everyone started talking at once, and the officers tried to shush them. Coral couldn't see the officers but remembered how different they looked in their dressing gowns than their uniforms when they guided the girls into the trench. They were probably cold and miserable, too.

"At the start of each year, just after Christmas, we go to Parkdale and camp by the beach for two weeks."

Camping at the beach? That sounded so lovely, and a million times better than the cold mud that squished through Coral's toes.

"So, for the ones who've already been, what's your favourite part?" Allison spoke her question into the dark and as there was no way of knowing who had hands up, they all spoke at once, intermingled with stern hushes from the officers, who didn't know who to blame for the noise.

"Prizes for the best kept tent!"

"Swimming!"

"Sand under my feet!"

"Concerts!"

"Building sandcastles!"

"Buying lollies at the shop!"

"Hush girls!" Rutter said. "With all your carry on, you'll be telling the enemy exactly where to find us!"

Her words terrified everyone into silence.

They sat in the cold and smelly mud until the officers were quite sure it was a drill and released them. Any mumbles were met with, "One day, girls, it might not be a drill. Today, we should give thanks it was."

Coral tried giving thanks just like they said, but it didn't make her feet any warmer.

Monday 22nd November, 1943—
Catherine Booth Home for Girls, East Kew

"Four eyes! Four eyes!"

There were so many things Coral could see now that she had new glasses. But that still didn't stop the sting of the teasing in the playground, especially from the younger girls.

Allison said not to worry about it, but Coral took to hiding her glasses in her pocket, and only took them out when she desperately needed them for school.

Mrs Paynter had this uncanny ability to write on the backboard and still be able to throw dusters and chalk at those talking or not paying attention. No matter how hard the girls tried to figure out how she was doing it, she still got it right most of the time. Coral wished she could use the flip top of her desk as a shield, but she was never quick enough. She was never quick enough for the ruler that came down on her left hand, either.

"We only write with our right hand Coral."

Her left hand often stung, and it reminded her of Mr Speight at Princes Hill. They must teach that kind of thing at Teacher's School. But if by magic, her hand hurt less every time someone hid a spider in Mrs Paynter's desk, or put a pin on her seat.

Mrs Paynter walked between the rows of desks as the girls worked on their compositions. As she got closer, Coral switched her pencil into her right hand.

"That's lovely handwriting Coral. It wouldn't surprise me if your service included some form of record keeping."

"My what, Mrs Paynter?"

"Your service, dear. When you go out to service."

Out to service. She'd heard it mentioned a few times, and Constance had told her some scary stories, but Coral thought she was just being like Violet; making up stories about the old, dilapidated house on the way to school. She didn't give it much heed. Now Mrs Paynter was telling her straight to her face that she'd be sent out to service.

"Did you hear me, Coral? What's that blank look on your face? You've gone such a funny pale shade; would you like to lie down for a bit?"

"But what would I do?"

"When?"

"When I go out to service."

"Why, everything we've taught you here, of course. Polishing floors and stairs, salting cups, making beds, kitchen work, ironing, washing, pegging out the washing. Darning socks, cleaning shoes. If you're to be a help, you must actually help, you know."

"So, I wouldn't be doing anything other than what I'm doing now?"

"I'm sure if your employer needs you for anything else, they'll teach you what to do."

Mrs Paynter patted Coral's shoulder, but Coral couldn't wipe the blank stare from her face. It was like it was stuck there.

"Be sure that you pay attention and learn quickly. You're meant to be a help to your employer, not a hindrance."

"And then what?"

"Then you stay with your employer's family until you're an adult."

"And then what?"

"Whatever your adult life brings you, Coral. Maybe you'll be a good enough girl to marry and become a solid member of the community. That's our aim, of course. Get you girls back on track after a rough start." She patted Coral's shoulder again. "Let's hope you do."

Coral didn't even know there *was* a track, let alone if she was on it or off it.

"Be industrious Coral. Do what you're told, and always be a good girl, and you'll have a terrific life with your employer."

Famished girls made their way into the dining room. They were never as serene as the officers hoped, but Coral thought they did quite well under the circumstances. She let out a little gasp and nudged Allison. "What did Constance *do*?"

Allison shrugged her shoulders. "Shh."

They were too far inside the dining room to risk talking, but Coral needed to know. Constance had obviously annoyed the officers again. Only the troublesome girls got the job of waiting on the officers, and for a whole month, too. When Coral caught her eye, she just rolled them, and thankfully did not get caught.

"Lights out!"

Just as the dormitory darkened, Coral remembered to ask Constance about having to serve at the officer's table.

She whispered as softly as she could. "Constance." When Constance didn't stir, she tried again, a bit louder, to bridge the gap between their beds. "Constance!"

Constance rolled over and faced her.

"What did you do to get waiting tables?"

The moonlight struck the glint in her eyes, and she smiled and stifled a giggle... "You know how we were meant to empty the potato water on the garden...?"

Coral giggled and couldn't wait for the story. "Tell me, tell me!"

A voice barked into the darkened dorm. "Coral Maxwell! No talking after lights out!" The officer's voice woke the sleepers and reignited the stirrers. Constance flipped her blanket over her head. "Out in the hallway now! You'll stand until I release you."

Coral had seen other girls get this punishment. Depending on who caught them, they might stand, kneel, or read aloud from the Bible in the draughty hallway. At first it wasn't so bad. But soon the warmth from her blankets evaporated from her body and her bare feet ached on the cold boards. All she wanted to do was get back into bed.

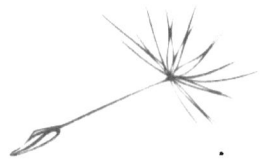

Sunday 26th December, 1943—
2/2nd Australian General Hospital via Atherton

Bert Maxwell entered the administration building of the 2/2nd Australian General Hospital Compound. The ten-minute walk across the base was uneventful, yet perspiration covered him. He doubted he'd ever get used to the tropical heat and humidity of the Atherton Tableland.

It was Corporal Taggert who'd sent for him and, after a brief wait, ushered him into a small office that was no cooler than outside. Louvered windows gave the assumption of a breeze, yet the only one came from a portable fan on his desk.

"Maxwell, looks like 1943 wasn't your year." He held a file with *'Maxwell. A.F Pte,'* written on the top right.

Bert stood to attention. "You could say that... Corporal."

Taggert flipped through his notes on his desk. "June it was, wasn't it? Conduct to the Prejudice of Good Order and Military Discipline. Fined 2 pound and confined to barracks for 14 days. By the Commanding Officer here at 2AGH?"

"Sounds about right."

Taggart glared a correction at him.

"I mean... Yes, Corporal."

"X-listed and sent here as medically fit for certain tasks, and then it seems, oh yes, here it is. Your hips and knees went. That's terrible luck, wouldn't you say?"

"Yes, Corporal."

"They've assigned you sedentary duties now. I'm sure that'll make you feel much better, won't it? Despite that, they have granted you proficiency pay, so that's something, I suppose."

"Yes, Corporal."

Taggart leant back in his chair and sighed. "Here's hoping 1944 is a better year for all of us."

"I'm hoping so. Yes, Corporal."

Saturday 22nd January, 1944—
Catherine Booth Home for Girls, East Kew

"Are you ready, girls?"

Major Bradbury wove her way through the excited arrangement of girls in their physical culture uniforms. Concerts were always thrilling, and they'd been practicing for absolute ages. The day was finally here.

Major Bradbury watched the girls most days when they practiced their gymnastics, ribbon dancing and bell ringing, offering them encouragement, and the girls would all try hard to impress her.

This year, the girls performed drills, songs, and exercises, with special performances from the senior, intermediate, and the junior girls. Quick costume changes made the two-hour show even more enjoyable.

Allison was particularly nervous. "Who—Who's out there?" she asked and tried to see the audience seated on chairs on the lawn in front of the home.

"Why Allison, there's the Mayor of Kew and the Mayoress and their friends. They've come to see the fine work you've been doing." Major Bradbury said. "And see there? That's Colonel Wescombe from the Salvation Army. He'll be giving out prizes and medals later."

"And the band?"

"They've come from Hawthorn, dear. Lots of people have come to see how well you're doing. Some are our patrons; they help keep the home running and this display makes them feel good inside. I hope it makes you feel good inside, too."

INSPECTOR'S REPORT
Wednesday 2nd February, 1944—
Catherine Booth Home for Girls, East Kew

Regarding Coral Maxwell (66420) born 13.09.1930, Inmate of the Salvation Army Girls Home, East Kew.

Coral seen on 21st January, 1944.

Tall and fair, with blue eyes. Teeth in good order.

Nice normal girl in Grade 6.

Clean and suitably clad when seen.

Matron said that the girl has written several times to her father.

Wednesday 3rd January, 1945—St. Kilda Road, Melbourne

"It's a shame you've been so… unwell, Private Maxwell."

Bert remained stoic as the clerk at the Victoria Barracks thumbed through his files. He was tired of moving from place to place while they found light duties work for him, or from hospital to hospital with the system. But it was almost over. So close he could just about taste it. Over for *him* anyway, while he waited his turn, he'd snuck a look at The Age the guy next to him was reading. One hundred and ninety-three Nazi planes had been shot down after they'd attempted a raid in England. Lincolnshire or somewhere. Oh well, not his problem.

"Best for everyone that you get a move on, don't you think?"

"If you believe so. You're the clerk."

"Hmph. You've spent the last year under the duress of osteoporosis; before that it was your feet."

"Yes, my body has been an unexpected and intolerable burden."

"I'm sure it has."

The stamp came down with a satisfying thud. 'Discharged' and a weight lifted from Bert's shoulders.

"Sign here." The clerk pointed at a piece of paper. "Here's your active service badge, for all that time you spent in Palestine." He had one eyebrow raised, but Bert didn't care.

"I'm a civilian again?"

"You are. And I wish you all the best with your injuries Mr Maxwell."

Tuesday 13th March, 1945—
C.W.D. Flinders Street Railway Building

"War does strange things to the minds of men." Mr Oxford let out a sigh that wasn't meant to be audible but needed expression.

Mrs Shaw continued her note taking among the softened whir of typewriters in the offices either side of them. "That it does."

He picked up his fountain pen, put it back down, and sighed again.

"What's brought on this melancholy?"

"Oh, that Maxwell chap."

"Any news?"

"Not yet. I've just had to send a letter through to the Footscray police to see if he'll talk to them about paying for his children. He obviously doesn't want to talk to us."

"But I thought you spoke to him on the telephone?"

"That was a month ago. He said he was employed at the Brooklyn Steel Works and earning 5 pound and 10 shillings a week. Fair enough, two shillings of that of that pays for his board, and he said he'd be quite prepared to pay 30 shillings per week for the children backdated from the end of January."

"Since then?"

"Nothing."

"At least he returned your call, I suppose."

"Probably got sick of my messages. Took us long enough to get his address after he was discharged. I'm glad he did. Now, we have to wait and see what the police can do for these children."

"What did you write?"

He pulled the paper from his typewriter and read,

The Officer in charge of police
Footscray

Re; Albert Maxwell, of Southampton Street Footscray.

The abovenamed, who was recently discharged from the Military Forces, is the father of three children who are wards of this department.

Maxwell agreed on the 19th ulto. to contribute 30/- per week towards their maintenance but up to date has not made one payment although I communicated with him twice on the matter.

I should be glad if the Officer in Charge would allow a Constable to interview him and ascertain why he has failed to keep his agreement. I should like him informed that if arrears are not paid at once and regular payments made in future, it is my intention to take the necessary action through the Court to see that he carries out his obligation.

Dulcie Shaw nodded. "I'd say that covers it."

"And now we wait."

Thursday 15th March, 1945—Southampton Street, Footscray

R.A. Hamilton, 1st Constable 7701 from the Footscray West Police, swung the low gate at the front of the house on Southampton Street, Footscray. The place looked neat enough, with a couple of plants along the short pathway.

His short and sharp knocks to the front door produced shuffling noises before the door opened to a middle-aged man, tired, but in good health.

"Good morning, Sir, I am Constable Hamilton from the Footscray West police needing to make an enquiry regarding Mr Albert Maxwell."

The man in front of him scratched at his head. "I'm Albert Maxwell. What's this about?"

"May I come in?"

"'Course."

Constable Hamilton tucked his helmet under his arm and entered through the hallway into a small lounge room, furnished with a striped couch and a side table covered with old newspapers and an empty beer bottle.

"I have with me a file from the children's welfare department. Now it appears that the promises you've made to the department in regard to the care and maintenance of your children haven't been honoured and they've asked me to attend and interview you as to the reasons for this delay."

"Oh I see," Bert rubbed at his whiskered chin, "Yes, of course. No harm Constable Hamilton, you see I've been working so hard I haven't had a chance to get into their offices. I'm at the steelworks, you see. Long hours and tough work."

"I'll bet. So, it's a matter of time and convenience, is it then?" He said as he flipped open his notepad.

"Yes, and being tired, of course. Look, I'll make an earnest effort at the end of the week. I will definitely call at their offices this Saturday."

Constable Hamilton looked around the room and stepped toward a calendar hanging on the wall. "The 17th of March then?"

Bert looked over his shoulder to confirm the date. "Yep, that's it. This Saturday, the 17th."

"Where you'll definitely attend to the matter?"

"My oath."

"Well then, Mr. Maxwell, I'll consider this interview completed and be on my way."

Bert followed Constable Hamilton to the door, "Thanks for your time, Constable."

Tuesday 24th April, 1945—
C.W.D. Flinders Street Railways Building

Mr Oxford put the letter into the outgoing mail tray with a weary sigh. He didn't even know what to think anymore.

Was it war or people or systems or all of it entwined that let these kids down? For now though, he welcomed a touch of respite; it was out of his hands.

To the Officer in Charge of Police
West Footscray

The attached papers refer to Coral, Allan and Ronald MAXWELL, who are wards of this department. I have endeavoured unsuccessfully to induce the father, Albert Maxwell, to contribute towards their maintenance.

I should be glad therefore if proceedings be instituted under Section 45 of the Children's Welfare Act with a view to securing an order against him. If I be advised of the date of hearing of the matter an officer from this department will attend the court. The authority for the police to prosecute is published in the government gazette of 29.09.1943, p. 2410

Secretary

Tuesday 22nd May, 1945—Footscray Local Court

The gavel banged in a simple crisp note.
It was done.

It was a month to the day that police instituted proceedings against Albert Maxwell for deserting his children and provided him with a summons to appear.

An order was made against him in his absence, for 10 shillings per week for each child.

A member of the Children's Welfare Department attended and prosecuted on the children's behalf.

INSPECTOR'S REPORT
Tuesday 26th June, 1945—
Catherine Booth Home for Girls, East Kew

Annual Inspection
Child seen is small for her age with nice fair hair and blue eyes. Still has trouble with bed wetting.
Helps with housework.
Was clean and suitably clad when seen.

Signed,
Inspector

Wednesday 15th August, 1945— Catherine Booth Home for Girls, East Kew

"Hurry girls, hurry!" "Mr Curtin is going to make an announcement on the radio."

"Who's Mr Curtin?"

"The prime minister dummy."

"Now, now, girls. Come in, come in quickly." Adjutant Tait called to all as she bent over and made sure the wireless was plugged in and working correctly.

What a treat! The girls packed into the dining room like sardines, eager to hear anything from the radio that was more than muffled sounds from the officer's rooms.

"We can't fit!" Some older girls cried, and Matron Bradbury whisked them off to her office to listen there.

Coral was squished into a corner but could see the top left corner of the wireless, its polished wood catching the light and showing the curves of its case.

"Shh! Shh! It's starting!" someone called, and a room full of giggly girls fell eerily silent as they strained to hear the crackling voice that came through the speaker.

Fellow citizens, the war is over.

The Japanese Government has accepted the terms of surrender imposed by the Allied Nations and hostilities will now cease. The reply by the Japanese Government to the note sent by Britain, the United States, the USSR and China, has been received and accepted by the Allied Nations.

At this moment, let us offer thanks to God.

Let us remember those whose lives were given that we may enjoy this glorious moment and may look forward to a peace which they have won for us.

Coral couldn't hear any more over the cheering and whooping. Even the little ones joined in; and they didn't even know what it all meant. The officers were jubilant, weary, and relieved. Matron Bradbury wiped a small tear from the corner of her eye. "Out and play girls! No school or chores today!" Coral felt the roof might lift off with all their cheering.

<u>Saturday 3rd November, 1945—
Catherine Booth Home for Girls, East Kew</u>

"Get the doctor! Get the doctor!"

It was the way the usually stoic Adjutant Tait made her voice boom through the hallways that put the girls immediately on edge. The whispers started straight away; she'd just been in Matron Bradbury's room.

Scores of panicked girls ran in different directions, but Coral stayed perfectly still at the back of the yard near the garden school. Watching and waiting, and wishing there was someone like Ronald to take care of; to take her mind off everything and to stop the lump in her throat from strangling her. Her tummy felt the same when they'd called for the doctor to tend to Mr Reynold.

A charge of girls ran to the house and were quickly sent out; their whispers rolled like a wave from the staircase to the backdoor, across the yard and to the corner where Coral now sat against the fence. It *was* Matron Bradbury.

Commands to *'stay outside'* rolled in shortly after, followed by, *'stay at the bottom of the stairs'* and *'don't get in the way.'*

'The doctor's here.'

Girls stepped back from the building and called to Matron Bradbury's room upstairs. "Please Doctor, make her better."

Another group of girls dropped to their knees near the pine trees and prayed.

'They're taking her now.'

The whispers rolled in, louder and more urgent, and girls cried openly.

An awful feeling moved from Coral's tummy to her chest, and bile rose in her throat. The flowers in the garden reminded her of Mrs Watson, but she knew she wouldn't arrive to take her hand and tell her everything will be fine. This time, she was on her own.

Older girls rounded up the crying ones. Some offered cuddles and reassurance, some just told them to shut up.

Coral picked a dandelion growing in the fence and fiddled with it, concentrating on all the little seeds. If she was tiny enough, she could hold onto one of the seeds and be blown completely away from all of this.

Allison turned up at her side. "What you gonna wish for?"

"I dunno. Not worth wishing for anything, is it?"

Coral blew the dandelion seeds free, and Allison brushed away the ones the breeze brought her way. Coral's wish lay scattered around her in the dirt of the garden paths. "Did you hear anything new?"

Allison slid down the fence and sat with a plop next to her. "I think she's dead. They all look so grim, don't they? Some girls say we should pray harder, but the doctor didn't look too pleased at all. Yep. I think she's dead."

"I do too."

The clouds brushed across the sky, unconcerned at the fate of the little girls below. "So, what will happen now, Coral?"

"I don't know. New matron I suppose."

"Hope she's nice."

Constance strode over. "Who's nice?"

Allison shielded her eyes from the sun. "The new matron, if we get one."

"You won't have to worry too much, anyway. You're just about to go out to service, like Faye did. I'm older. I'll be off first, then Allison, then you."

Faye left a few weeks ago. Off to her 'new life,' she called it. Coral sighed. "I Suppose. Mrs Paynter said it's just like being here and doing all the work we do here, but somewhere else."

"Kinda"

"Well, what's different?"

"You'll be with a family for a start."

A family? Like the Reynolds again? "That sounds nice."

"If you get a nice family, that is."

Coral had never thought about families not being nice. Then her cheeks flushed. She felt like an idiot; so many new girls came with bruises and nightmares, and Matron Bradbury would hold them and rock them to sleep with tears in her eyes. Of course, there were unkind families. *What would she do if she got sent to an unkind family?* "I'd leave."

"Yeah, you can't, though. Some girls have even run away and come back here. They weren't treated right by the lady of the house. And sometimes," she whispered, "by the man of the house ... or his sons."

Coral imagined Constance whispered because it must be much worse, because boys could hit harder.

She continued. "But if the girls run away, they get sent to a reform school."

"What's that?"

"Like a jail for girls."

Coral's fear made her vocal and frustrated. "That can't be right, Constance! So, you're saying... the people..."

"Employers."

"The employers do something wrong or hurt the girls, and the girls run away, and because they run away, they get sent to jail?"

"Not much of a choice, is it? Stay with the horrible people or go to jail."

"And they beat us?"

"There's stuff worse than beating—"

Coral frowned.

"Girls, girls, gather round."

Adjutant Tait stood on the back step and called the girls to make an announcement. Constance, Allison, and Coral rose to join the throng, fully aware of what the announcement was about.

Coral instinctively placed her arms around the shoulders of the younger girls beside her, and they leant their heads into her and wept.

Adjutant Pearl Tait spoke with tender words, and Coral wondered how it was possible to feel all alone in a mansion, surrounded by so many people. But this place was not her home. Maybe it was *out there* somewhere, and she'd find it when she got sent out to service.

What if it's not a good home?

Coral's eyes widened at the thought. What *would* she do then? Stay and be unfairly punished? Or run away and be punished? The lump in her throat grew as she watched someone pulling the curtains closed in Matron Bradbury's room. She'd miss her beautiful singing voice the most, and how she changed those horrible navy uniforms into different coloured floral dresses for the girls.

And now she wasn't here to answer any of Coral's questions.

This new home she was being sent to; what if they died on her too?

Vale Matron Bessie Bradbury.

Coral could hear the beautiful and soothing words that Adjutant Tait used in her prayer, and she said '*Amen*' at the end, like all the other girls, but she wasn't really listening to any of it. She heard it, but she didn't listen.

It was the first time she realised you could do those two things together. They only seem the same but are actually very different.

Friday 14th December, 1945— Catherine Booth Home for Girls, East Kew

Irene Fishwick wasn't any more pleasant as a matron than she was as the Major in charge of the laundry. The new matron was as opposite to Matron Bradbury as you could get. Tall and thin, she had long grey hair that she plaited and wound around her head and sneered at the girls from behind her glasses. She'd locked Coral in the cupboard one time for punishment; and then forgot her until teatime.

Her second-in-charge, Adjutant Rutter, was just as mean. She had short dark hair and a shrill voice that cut through the air like the sharpest knife in the kitchen. Life was so very different after Matron Bradbury passed away.

Fishwick and Rutter worked as a team and had terrifying conversations around the girls.

"Yes, Matron Fishwick," Rutter would say, "Control these girls' bodies, and you control their minds. Their lives must be regimented!"

"I agree Adjutant Rutter. Strictness controls the mind. Discipline the mind to help secure compliance of the body."

"They will thank us, you know. In due course."

"Punishments are proven to conform these wayward girls into productive members of our society."

At times when Coral sat in the dark in the huge cupboard, she wondered if they'd deliberately made the linen cupboard so big to fit all the girls in. She hated the dark and being alone. Not as much as it terrified the tiny ones. How she felt for them when they screamed in terror at being locked away. But for her, it was better than the cane, or reciting bible passages in the cold hallways. At least she could close her eyes and be anywhere in the world inside the cupboard.

Allison had already left for service, swallowed up by the big bad world, and Coral had no idea where she was.

Constance was due to leave the next day. She was going to a place called Mia Mia. It was out in the bush somewhere.

"You know why they call it Mia Mia?" she asked and then chuckled as she replied to Coral's shrug. "I I don't don't know know."

Coral laughed at her silliness and wished with every bone in her body Constance would find a nice family. If they hadn't been lying in their beds, she would have searched for a dandelion to make it so.

"Coral, everything starts new for me tomorrow," she whispered. "And for you too, soon enough. Just think, you can be anyone you want. You don't have to be '*Coral the Homie from the Salvos*' anymore. Never know, I might become '*Connie, the best horsewoman in Victoria*'. Don't see it as the end of this. See it as the beginning." She sat up on one elbow. "First up safety. If you're safe, be whoever you want, don't let the bitches here—"

"Lights out!"

Coral knew why she dropped on to her back and stopped talking. Rutter would take great delight punishing Constance harshly on her very last night.

Saturday 15th December, 1945—
Catherine Booth Home for Girls, East Kew

And just like that, Constance was gone.

The ache in Coral's heart demanded she stop making attachments. Stop being friends. That way, she won't get hurt when they leave.

Like they all left.

She grunted as she flipped her mattress that morning.

Flip.

Everything flips.

Mattresses flip, coins flip.

Everyone's days and lives flip in an instant here, and she didn't get a say in any of it. Even when it was about her.

Coral flopped onto her bare mattress and expected Rutter's shrill screech in her ear at any moment, but she didn't care anymore.

Can't wait to get out of here and into Service!

But I'll be alone.

Who'll have my back?

Will the family take care of me?

Where's Dad?

... and what's worse than being beaten?

Monday 21st January, 1946—
Catherine Booth Home for Girls, East Kew

Matron Fishwick's black shoes stopped right in Coral's view and distracted her from cleaning the skirting boards in the long hallway. She didn't need to see the shoes to know it was Fishwick. The officers all had different walks, and it was best to know who was coming before they arrived. Her predicament was whether she should stop cleaning and respectfully pay attention, lest she get the cane; or should she keep cleaning and to save from her from the cane for laziness? There were no right decisions anymore. She kept cleaning.

"I've written your last review for you," Fishwick said. Her tone was smug, and Coral had already learnt it best not to speak unless she asked you to. She kept cleaning as Fishwick continued. "Ready for your prospective employers, you see. It's quite simple, just like you. It says you've been here for almost 3 years, you're good for housework and manual labour. Conduct... hmm, I rated you as adequate. Not bright mentally, but otherwise in good health. Sound fair to you?"

Coral quietly cleared her throat, "Yes, Matron," and scrubbed at the same scuff mark on the skirting over and over and listened to Fishwick's footsteps soften in the distance.

Fishwick makes the choice of where I go?
Heaven help me.
I have to make it out there, or go to jail.
Good or a bad doesn't even matter; I still don't get any choices.

Coral sat with her back against the wall, the cleaning cloth still clenched in her hand and muttered through her teeth.

"Bugger! ..... Double bloody bugger! What am I to do now?"

Tuesday 5th February, 1946—
C.W.D. Flinders Street Railway Building.

Mrs Hughes, "Highfields" Jeetho, an old employer requires the services of a girl—she has been communicated with re–Coral. Her reply awaits.

Wednesday 6th February, 1946—
C.W.D. Flinders Street Railway Building.

Mrs. Hughes called. Placement to be made 8th February 1946.

Wages 17 shillings and 6 pence per week, and savings set aside from that amount of 2 shillings and 6 pence per week.

Mrs Hughes will call at this office on Friday to collect Coral and her wages book.

Jeetho

1946

Thursday 7th February, 1946—
Catherine Booth Home for Girls, East Kew

Coral's head spun. Thank goodness it was Adjutant Tait who gave her the instructions about her service kit. If it was Rutter or Fishwick, she'd be so flustered she wouldn't hear anything. The other girls were in school, so it was just the two of them at her bed in the dorm. They hovered over a small beaten-up suitcase.

"Now, here's your kit," Tait began and handed items for Coral to place inside the case. "You'll be signing for all this, and if you ruin any of these things or they need to be replaced, you will be the one paying for them."

"Me?"

"You'll be receiving a wage, remember?"

"Oh that's right."

"Your employer will pay your wages and keep some money aside on your behalf. They'll send it to the Children's Welfare Office for your savings. Now, I'll read these things out, you check off that you have them. Two aprons, two pairs of shoes, three nightdresses, three vests, one slip, four dresses, one pair of hose, 3 pairs of pantlettes, two pairs of socks, one hat, one cardigan, one coat, one suitcase."

"All here." Coral gave a quick nod. None of the clothes were new, but that didn't matter at all. She had her own 'things' at last. Coral bit her bottom lip, "Adjutant Tait?"

"Yes Coral?"

"Do you know where I'm going?"

"A place in the country, it's called Jeetho."

"There's less people in the country, isn't there?"

Tait nodded, "Less people, and that means more space for you."

They both looked around at the dorm crammed full of beds, and Coral twisted and pulled at her fingers. "I've never been to the country before."

"Well, there'll be lots of open space if you're on a farm."

"Open space? Like at Royal Park?"

"Yes, just like that. Only it goes as far as the eye can see." Adjutant Tait clipped the suitcase shut and placed it beside Coral's bed. "Be a good girl, Coral, and everything will be fine, you'll see. Try to get some sleep tonight; tomorrow's your big day."

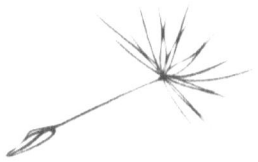

Friday 8th February, 1946—
C.W.D. Flinders Street Railway Building

Janet didn't mind the long walk down the hallway to Mrs Shaw's office. It was nice to get away from the reception desk for a while, and Mrs Shaw always had a ready smile for her. She knocked, waited for Mrs Shaw's 'yes' and pushed the door open.

"Mrs Hughes is here to see you."

"Thank you, Janet. You can bring her right in."

Dulcie Shaw greeted Mrs Hughes as she entered. Even though Mrs Hughes had employed girls as domestics before, this was their first meeting. A tall, slim woman, Dulcie liked her immediately. She seemed to have an air of calm about her; something every ward of the state needed but was rarely afforded.

Once they'd exchanged their pleasantries, Mrs Shaw gestured towards her desk and the chairs waiting for them. "So, we've just the paperwork to organise. I see you've had a service girl before, so there's no need to go over the contract again. If you could just read this agreement and confirm it's all correct by signing at the bottom, there."

Mrs Hughes popped her hat on the desk while she read. It was a pretty hat, perhaps new and daintier than Mrs Shaw thought a farmer's wife would wear. Yet, her work had taught her that people were always full of surprises.

Mrs Hughes held the pre-printed form with Coral's file number; 66420 typed distinctly at the top of the page. The title, 'Service Agreement' ran in large bold letters across its width and the correct pronouns, dates, and amounts had been typed into the allowed spaces.

To the Secretary
Children's Welfare Department,
Flinders St, Melbourne.

CORAL MAXWELL a ward of the state, entered my employment on **FRIDAY** the **8**[th] Day of **FEBRUARY** 19 **46**, and I agree
(1) To pay **her** wages at the rate of **17/6** per week for the first three months;
(2) at the end of that period to consider the question of an increase;
(3) to forward quarterly to your office, to be banked for **her**, a portion of such wages at the rate of **2/6** per week;
(4) to pay the balance to **her**, taking a receipt for each payment in the book provided for the purpose by the Department, and to see as far as possible that the sums so paid are judiciously expended by **her**, on suitable and necessary clothing, &c., so that the kit shall be kept up at all times to the full value of the outfit originally received; and
(5) to comply with the Service conditions as printed on the back hereof.

I have received a copy of this agreement.

Mrs Hughes signed the document. "Is that all you need from me today? That didn't take long at all."

"Well, it's all about records and signatures these days, isn't it? Are you travelling back to Jeetho today?"

Mrs Hughes nodded. "We came in yesterday for my husband to attend a Soldiers Settlement Committee meeting. Now it's off to Kew to collect the girl, and then we'll be on our way home."

The two ladies walked side by side to reception. "Well, at least you have nice weather for it. Safe travels."

"Thank you, Mrs Shaw."

Mrs Hughes tapped the elevator button just as Mrs Shaw spoke up. "Oh, and Mrs Hughes?"

"Yes?"

"We'll write to the Rationing Commissioner and ask them to expedite the issue of Coral's ration book and clothing coupon card."

"That will be helpful. Thank you again."

The elevator doors closed, and Mrs Shaw dropped her smile and rushed to her office. She had to type up that letter before she forgot.

Friday 8th February, 1946—
South Gippsland Highway, Victoria

Mrs Hughes stood at the bottom of the grand staircase at the Catherine Booth Home for Girls. Her small felt hat with embroidered flowers around the brim matched the little green flowers in her dress. Coral wondered if there'd be flowers on the farm. She thought about flowers all the way down the stairs, all the names she could remember, all the colours she could think of. It was the only way to stop her legs from wobbling, and her hands from dropping the suitcase.

"Good morning, Coral," Mrs Hughes's voice was clear and crisp.

"Good morning," Coral replied, but hers sounded weak and squeaky.

"I see you're all packed. Shall we go to the car?"

Coral nodded and left her home. Just like Allison, just like Constance. She walked through the solid green door for the last time.

"This is my husband, Mr Hughes."

Mr Hughes seemed kind. He smiled and nodded at Coral as she climbed into the back seat with her suitcase. "Would you like to put your case in the boot[1]?" he asked.

Mrs Hughes spoke before Coral had a chance. "Don't worry, Mr Hughes. There's plenty of room back there, and I think Coral would prefer her things close by. Isn't that right, Coral?"

---

1. Trunk

Coral didn't know what she thought, or what she was supposed to do, so she smiled a little and that seemed enough for Mrs Hughes.

At first, the drive was like any other. There were houses, and shops, and service stations[2], and then the gaps between them became larger and wider. The sky was all dreary and cloudy when they'd left, and now there were patches of blue stretching out wider from the clouds. It was like everything was opening up and nothing was like it was before. Adjutant Tait was right; it was open as far as the eye could see.

Mrs Hughes wore her brown hair in a neat bun that clipped and bobbed against the back of her seat when she turned to talk to Mr Hughes. Mr Hughes had half dark hair, half grey hair, kind of like the old Labrador that lived next door to the Home. They seemed nice, but many people she'd met seemed nice at first. How far did those other girls have to run? Did they get taken this far away? She wouldn't even know where to start because she had no idea where she was!

The motion of the car almost rocked her off to sleep. She awoke with a start and reminded herself to be awake in case something interesting happened. But it didn't.

The car slowed and pulled off the road into a wayside rest stop.

"Here we are," Mrs Hughes said. "Time for some lunch." The thought of lunch made Coral's tummy growl.

"Out you get Coral. The toilets are over there, and once we've had lunch, we'll stretch our legs with a brisk walk on the jetty."

"Where are we?" Coral could smell salt water and the surrounding plants looked all twisted and warped.

"Tooradin. We often stop here on our way to and from Melbourne."

By the time Coral returned, Mrs Hughes had arranged sandwiches wrapped in paper on a picnic rug. Mr Hughes undid the thermos and poured them all a cup of tea. Coral sat in the spare space, opened her sandwich, and took a large bite.

---

2. Gas stations

"Goodness, look at you go." Mrs Hughes said, "There's plenty of food for hardworking girls on the farm."

Coral *had* bitten a large piece of her sandwich. She didn't realise there was meat and chutney inside. She didn't care too much for the chutney, but after so many years of vegemite, peanut butter, or jam, her sandwich tasted like heaven. It just took her a long time to chew it all and answer politely. "It's very delicious, Mrs Hughes, thank you."

On the highway, cars continued to pass them as they ate together. It was a very grown-up thing, she thought, to be sitting by the side of the road, sipping tea, and eating meat and chutney sandwiches on a picnic rug. The people driving past would think they were a family. But they weren't. It was kind of like a secret, when what you present to others is different from what is really going on.

They folded the picnic rug and tucked it away in the boot. "Come on, you stragglers!" Mr Hughes called. He was already walking his way along the bank of the inlet.

All three of them walked the jetty alone with their own thoughts. The wind battered their ears so badly it was hard to hear anybody, anyway. It'd be lovely to live by the bay. Crabs shuffled in and out of their little holes along the tide line in the inlet. The sand seemed different here. Smelly and sodden; not like the sandy beaches at Parkdale. And there were weird plants. They stuck straight up out of the sand. Mr Hughes said they were called mangroves. No one had ever told her there were different kinds of beaches, different kinds of families, different kinds of everything.

"Ah, it's good to be home." Mrs Hughes turned her head to check on Coral. The car had slowed and turned up a small dirt road. Only the dirt road was their driveway. Much longer than the one at East Kew, it wound alongside a gully and led to a homestead on top of a hill. There were views into the valley below. Steep green grassed hills with cattle grazing here and there. Coral stepped out of the car and was almost bowled over by the wind that blew up the valley, over the top of them, and continued on its way.

Mr Hughes gathered some items from the car and stopped next to her on his way to the house. "Well, what do you think?"

It smelt odd. It must be the animals, but she didn't want to tell him his farm stinks. That would be impolite. "It's very windy up here."

"That it is."

"And it's... different."

"There'll be lots of different things here, but you're a smart girl, you'll get used to it."

Mr Hughes continued on his way but a young man in muddy pants and braces stopped him in his tracks. He put his hand up to the young man and interrupted what he was about to say, even though the young man's mouth was wide open. "This is Coral, your mum's new girl."

The young man nodded in Coral's direction.

Mr Hughes handed some of his items to the impatient man, still not allowing him to speak. "And this is our son, Kenny. He'd only be a couple of years older than you."

Kenny was sick of waiting. "The fencing wire in the bottom paddock[3] has tangled and is in a right mess. I need a hand."

"Let me get these things inside first. I'll meet you there."

And with that, Kenny was gone.

Mrs Hughes passed Coral on her way into the house. "The life of farmers," she said.

Coral followed Mrs Hughes into the grand house, through the ballroom and into her own little room. "You can pop your suitcase in here."

At first, Coral thought there must be some kind of mistake. Her room had a polished timber bedhead, a floral bedspread, a carpet for her feet in the morning, and a lamp beside her bed so she could read at night. She even had her own fireplace. Coral carefully opened the wardrobe and all the drawers in the dresser. They were empty, of course, ready for her things.

---

3. Field

"Ready?" Mrs Hughes called from the hallway.

Coral hadn't put anything away yet, but she could always do that later. She hurried out into the hallway.

"Good. Let's get to work."

Coral peeled the potatoes while Mrs Hughes set about warming up some cold meat she took out of the icebox. It looked like roast meat. Might've been the meat that was on their sandwiches. Coral's tummy growled again. That chutney wasn't so bad after all.

'Highfields'.

It certainly kept up to its name.

What a strange summer they were having. Cold mornings and very hot days.

The homestead was very high up, and when the wind wasn't sweeping its way up the cleared mountainside, it was blowing across the face of the property, bringing those unseasonally cold winds, straight from the bay.

The iron roof of the chook shed[4] rattled, and Coral ducked just in case.

Kenny chuckled somewhere outside the shed. He must've seen. "It's coming from the bay this morning."

"How can you tell?"

"I reckon I can smell a hint of salt in the air. Dad thinks I'm loopy, but the bay's only about 10 miles that way. It even warms up a bit as it crosses the land."

"It's colder at the beach?"

"Too right."

Coral reached under an unimpressed hen. Delightful warmth snuggled her fingers. She'd definitely changed her mind. There was no way she want-

---

4. Chicken coop

ed to live near the bay now. The crack of Kenny's axe splitting firewood reminded her she had fireplaces to clean. Fourteen of them!

She closed the chook shed door behind her and trotted back to the house.

"Where are you off to in such a hurry?" Kenny called after her.

"Out of this bloody wind!"

Saturday 23rd February, 1946—'Highfields', Jeetho

I can be anyone. Just like Constance said.

Coral played with the pen in her hand while Mrs Hughes found the wages book in the polished bureau.

"Each week, we'll perform this same ritual, Coral. I'll present you with your wages, you check the amount and sign your name to say you've received them. It's good training for what goes on in the world. You must always check details before signing anything."

"Yes, Mrs Hughes," Coral looked at the 15 shillings in her hand - what a windfall! She'd already decided on her new name and signed in her best handwriting... *Gladys Maxwell*.

"And yes," Mrs Hughes intuited, "We'll go into town today. But don't be silly with your money. I have to record how you've spent it for the department."

Coral meant to say *'Yes, Mrs Hughes.'* but what came out was a garbled "Yaaayhs" that made Mrs Hughes laugh and shake her head.

The General Store in Loch kept much of what anyone might need. Coral felt most grown up doing her own shopping. She carried the basket Mrs Hughes had lent to her in front and wandered along the display cases and shelves, looking at everything, even though she already knew what she wanted to buy. She needed an apron; one that fit her properly, so she didn't have to wear Mrs Hughes' big old tea towel stuffed into her belt. And socks! How could *all* her socks get wet, and take so long to dry?

Mr Barker worked out how much she should pay, and wrapped her goods in brown paper while she collected her coins from a small purse Mrs Hughes had given to her.

Mrs Hughes arrived next to her at the counter with a basket much fuller than Coral's. "I'm almost finished here, Coral. Would you please go to the post office and buy three stamps for me? It's a short walk across the road. See it just there?" With that, she dropped 8 pence into Coral's hand and turned back to Mr Baker.

The Post Office was pretty, as far as buildings go. Its large open foyer had community announcements about dances and farm sales pinned to its walls, but Coral imagined people gathered there for a chat on windy days.

Coral stood on the footpath and watched people come and go through the door. Women smiled and men nodded as they saw her there, but she couldn't bring herself to enter.

"Come along, Coral!" Mrs Hughes called from outside the General Store. "Did you get my stamps?"

"Not yet."

"Why ever not?" Mrs Hughes marched towards her, "They can't be closed." People moved in and out of the post office and answered Mrs Hughes query, which added to her confusion. "Why haven't you bought my stamps?"

Coral watched her feet shuffle against each other. "I don't know how to buy a stamp."

"You what?... pardon?"

"They didn't teach us things like that at the Home. The only reason I knew how to shop was I stayed with a lady when I was little and saw how shops work." Coral sniffled.

"Now, now, young lady. That's enough of that. How will you ever learn if you don't get to do it for yourself? Let's go into the Post Office together. You ask for what you would like, and pay for it, just like at the General Store. I will stand nearby to help you if you get confused."

Coral wiped at her nose. "Alright."

"Remember to speak clearly. You've as much right to buy a stamp as anyone else."

There wasn't a queue when they entered, and Mrs Hughes pointed to where she should wait until called.

"Next please."

"Hello. May I have three 2 ½ pence stamps please?"

"You certainly can." The postmaster tore off some stamps from a page in a big flat book. "You're new around here, aren't you? Where are you staying?"

Coral checked behind her for Mrs Hughes's support. "At Highfields."

"With the Hughes family, of course. How are you, Eileen?"

"Very well Ted. We'll be off home now."

"Good-o. Say g'day to Joseph for me."

"Will do."

Wednesday 27th February, 1946—'Highfields', Jeetho

"I'm heading to the store this morning; you can come once you've finished polishing the sitting room furniture."

"I'm almost done!" Coral called.

She tried to make a memory in her head, one she wouldn't forget, about asking Mrs Hughes if she needed stamps today. She could do that now. And so many other things she'd learnt from Eileen Hughes.

It must be because she was a schoolteacher, that's why she had so many rules, and why Coral tried so hard not to break them; like always having your shoes polished. Sometimes she was so terrified she'd do something wrong; she'd wait to be told what to do. Then they wouldn't send her away, she reasoned, because she hadn't done anything wrong.

Mrs Hughes peeled her vegetables differently to how they were taught in the home, and Coral soon understood, *different was wrong*. Mrs Hughes swept the same though. She pegged clothes differently, and explained if we wore it on the top, hang it from the bottom, and if it's worn on the bottom, hang it from the top. That was easy to remember. Mrs Hughes's garden was way more important than gardens ever were at the Home. Probably because the Home grew flowers, Mrs Hughes grew vegetables.

Of all the vegetables and flowers that grew at Highfields, Coral liked the rosebush outside her bedroom window the best. There were lots of open blooms, and some half opened and one little bud hiding behind the bush where it couldn't be seen. Sometimes she wished she was that little bud, hiding and never getting into trouble.

Coral quickly washed her hands and changed her clothes, ready to visit the General Store.

"What will you be buying today?" Mrs Hughes asked as they drove into Loch.

"I need a new jumper[5], and a couple of other small things."

On the top of Coral's 'other small things' list, was new shoe polish.

Friday 22nd March, 1946— 'Highfields', Jeetho

Another day, another fireplace.

Mrs Hughes rested on the lounge and flipped through Coral's copy of *The Woman's Weekly*. "I do love that you're such an avid reader, Coral. You know you can borrow any of the books I have in my library. Just remember to ask first."

"Thank you, Mrs Hughes." Coral used the old dustpan and brush to scrape out the ash and wood from the fireplace. She was extra careful not to get ash on the carpets. "I like the stories that continue with each issue best."

"The serials."

"Yes, that's what they're called." Now it was time to scrub inside with the stiff bristled broom. She expected to clean these wretched fireplaces a lot during the winter, but they'd had what Mr Hughes called a 'cold snap' and

---

5. Sweater

had used the living room fireplace recently. Next, she gripped the pumice stone, dipped it in dish soap and scrubbed at the bricks surrounding the fireplace.

"What would you like me to do next?" Coral asked while she tidied her things.

Mrs Hughes rose and inspected the fireplace. "Really Coral, you can't see those streaks?" Her voice was quite firm, not angry... but almost. Coral squinted and opened her eyes wide, but still couldn't see what she was talking about. "I had a student like you once. They needed glasses. I think it best we telephone and find out when the next representative from Coles and Garrard will be in the area."

"Yes, Mrs Hughes." The thought of wearing glasses again depressed Coral, but she remembered how the screen in the picture theatre wasn't that clear when Mrs Hughes had dropped her there last week. Maybe it was for the best. Maybe grown-ups don't call each other 'four-eyes'. Maybe going to the pictures could be even *more* fun.

Some nights were so still and quiet. Coral listened to the crickets and heard the cows mooing in the deep valley. But most nights, the wind whistled and hummed around the house, and rattled and banged something squeaky in the distance.

"Go to sleep Coral," she'd tell herself, and then slap her hand hard. "Don't wet the bed, don't ruin it. You've found a nice family. Be good."

Friday 29th March, 1946—
C.W.D. Flinders Street Railway Building

Mrs Shaw held a letter in one hand and an open envelope in the other. "It's a letter from Mrs Hughes at Jeetho. She's included a cheque for Coral's first seven weeks of savings... She says Coral's settling in well and happily to their home. Oh, dear..."

"What?" Mr Oxford had stopped his work to listen, and didn't like the sound of Dulcie's *'Oh Dear'*

Mrs Shaw continued reading. "Her work has been handicapped by very poor eyesight. I took her to Coles and Garrard to be tested and she will receive glasses in a few weeks' time."

Mr Oxford sighed in relief. "I thought she might tell us something more awful than poor eyesight."

"Poor eyesight is a burden, Mr Oxford, particularly when the girls are expected to notice what needs cleaning."

"Very true."

"Listen to this.... She told me she previously wore glasses but when they were broken at the home at Kew they were not replaced. I'll give a more detailed report next quarter."

"Did you know Coral wore glasses?"

"I've never seen her wear them. Have you?"

Mr Oxford shook his head. "Surely there's something listed in the Inspector's Reports."

"Or at the Home itself."

INSPECTOR'S REPORT
Wednesday 10th April, 1946—'Highfields', Jeetho

SERVICE REPORT

Home is very good.

She has a comfortably furnished room in the house.

General housework, but no washing and a little cooking.

The girl seems happy, but the employer is having a little difficulty in training her.

The wages book is fine.

Healthy but is getting glasses as she is very short-sighted. Mrs Hughes has advanced cost of same.

The car is out of order, so they are unable to get to church up to date.

<u>Saturday 11th May, 1946—'Highfields', Jeetho</u>

The morning sun formed a strip of light on Coral's bedroom wall where the curtains *just* didn't meet. Saturday's jobs were to—

Ugh! She was wet. She knew it. No. No. No.

Coral flicked back her blankets and a horrifying gasp shut her throat.

Blood!

She was bleeding! Dying in fact! Dying because she did something wrong.

Be sure your sins will find you out! That's what they said at the Home, ... something about the blood of Christ.

Mrs Hughes couldn't see this!

She'd know.

Coral feverishly clawed at the sheets and pulled them from the bed. Her nightdress was stained, too. How could she wash them? She's not allowed to use the boiler.

The dam. She'd wash them in the dam.

And if they saw her, she could say she fell in.

With her sheets?

... No, that wouldn't work.

Coral hugged at her sheets. Bugger! There's blood on the mattress too. Tears stung her eyes and her heart thumped so hard it hurt.

Clothes. She needed to change her clothes! A quick turn knocked her lamp off the bedside table.

"Coral, what's going on?" Mrs Hughes came down the hallway.

Coral stuffed the sheets under her bed, pulled the blankets up over the mattress stain and stood by her bedside table when Mrs Hughes came into her room.

"I just knocked over my—"

"Coral!" Mrs Hughes barked and flung back her blankets. "What on earth is going on?"

She'd forgotten about her nightdress. It told her sinful tale. Coral burst into tears. "I don't *know!*" she wailed.

"They did tell you, didn't they, the officers at the Home?"

"Tell me what?"

"What this means."

Coral trembled, and her body wracked with sobs. "I've made a mess. I'm sinful, and dying. And you'll send me away now." Coral didn't want to cry but was too overwhelmed to keep it all in.

"Do they not teach you girls anything in that Home?"

Mrs Hughes was angry again, and Coral hugged herself.

"Good thing the men are already in the paddock. Off to the bathroom with you. I'll clean this while you wash up, then we'll have a cup of tea and a chat."

Coral sobbed quietly while she chose her clothes for the day.

"And Coral, we won't be sending you away."

Coral didn't mind the breeze on warmer days, or when it was gentle enough to sit on the front porch. She loved watching the train puff its way in and out of the Jeetho Station. From her seat, she could see the station rooftop at the bottom of the steep grassy hill in front of her. The trains came through every half an hour whistling when they left, hauling all sorts of goods towards either Leongatha or Melbourne.

Kenny came and stood on the porch next to her, crunching into an apple.

"Have you ever caught the train, Kenny?"

"Heaps of times."

"Really? It's such a long way to the station. Out to the highway and back in again."

"Don't be stupid. We go down the hill and step through the fence. Just there near the tree, see how it's a bit out of whack?"

"Where do you go?"

"Usually just the pictures at Korumburra. The Alpha Theatre. Been there?"

"Once I think. Your mum dropped me off for the matinee."

"We should go together one day."

"We should?"

"I'll let you know when I'm going next. There are some good pictures coming up. Melbourne gets them first, of course."

"Of course."

Kenny finished his apple and threw it into the garden. "Hoo roo[6], Coral."

"Hoo roo."

---

6. Goodbye

Monday 1st July, 1946—
C.W.D. Flinders Street Railway Building

Mrs Shaw unwrapped the scarf from her neck and placed her handbag on the floor by her desk. They should rename the streets of Melbourne wind tunnels, not streets; particularly in July. "Was that another letter from Mrs Hughes out at Jeetho that I saw this morning?"

John Oxford chuckled at her. "You don't miss a thing, do you? By the way, I've already dropped the cheque in with the bookkeeper."

"So, what's the news?" she asked and peeled her coat off and dressed the back of her chair with it.

"Nothing wonderful, but nothing horrendous, either. Mrs Hughes said Coral had made some improvement in her personal hygiene, but still has to make more determined efforts to combat her seemingly natural disregard for truth."

"What does that mean, exactly?"

"You could always write and ask for clarification if you want. Otherwise, she says Coral keeps well and is punctual, and she thinks she's capable of being responsive to her wishes for her general improvement."

"This is good news, really. There doesn't seem to be anything Mrs Hughes is finding disagreeable. Coral *has* found a wonderful home to be a part of."

Wednesday 10th July, 1946—'Highfields', Jeetho

Coral had finished the washing up, and replaced the dwindling soap inside its cage, when Kenny gave her the signal. Mrs Hughes was reading in the lounge room; and according to Kenny, this was the best time to approach her.

"Excuse me, Mrs Hughes," Coral began. "May I have some money to go to the pictures in Korumburra?"

"When were you planning to go?"

"This Saturday. They're playing the Fantasia Re-release, and I didn't get to see it when it first played."

Mrs Hughes rose to get her purse. "I could always lunch with Mrs Harris while I wait for you in town."

"I'd really like to go to the afternoon screening."

"But that would finish after dark Coral. I can't allow that."

Kenny popped his head around the corner. "I wouldn't mind seeing it again, Mum. I'll take Coral, and we'll catch the train, so you won't have to drive anywhere."

Mrs Hughes thought for a moment, weighing things up like her balancing kitchen scales. "Very well then. Here you are Coral, four shillings. I'll record it in your wages book, but don't be home too late."

"We won't," Kenny called from the hallway.

Saturday 13th July, 1946—'The Alpha Theatre', Korumburra

Kenny and Coral were still giggling when they arrived at the theatre. His pants had caught and ripped as they made their way through the fence and in unhooking it, they'd nearly missed their train.

Kenny passed his money to the lady working at the ticket office. "Ow, stop making me laugh; my sides hurt. 'Fantasia' please."

A loud guffaw caught both their attention. Two adults laughed together as they entered the theatre and caught both Coral and Kenny off guard.

Coral paid for her ticket, and they lined up for ice cream. "Your parents don't laugh much, do they?"

"Maybe parents just don't laugh."

"So, it's not me and my mistakes?"

"What? No, not at all. They've been like this for a while." Kenny paid for their ice creams. "Dad disappears. Mum pretends not to notice."

"It's weird when adults think you don't see things because you're a kid."

"In all honesty, it probably goes both ways."

Coral tried to think how that would work and got her mind in a tangle, so she shrugged her shoulders and licked at her ice cream.

Kenny chose seats at the back, took her hand and led her up the darkened aisle. She was glad no one could see the heated blush rising on her cheeks. It all felt a bit daring.

The newsreel was a boring thing about politics, so they whispered to each other to pass the time.

"Will you be okay?" Coral asked.

"What do you mean?"

"With your parents bickering, and not being themselves. It makes me feel awful inside, and they're not even my parents."

Kenny put his arm around Coral and she settled into the seat without a worry in the world. "No need to worry about us country boys. We're always beaut."

The movie was bright and colourful and made Coral appreciate her glasses more. There were many times she gasped with the wonder of it all. There were scenes of moving music and dancing toadstools, Mickey Mouse and strange unicorns dancing. At one point, she turned to see if Kenny was enjoying it too, and he gently touched her jaw and brought her lips to his. Her first kiss felt more special with all the beautiful music that surrounded her.

Kenny moved his hand toward her waist, and she pushed it away.

"Aw," he joked, "Why do you always have to be the good girl?"

"Just because," she smirked and took a moment to wonder that for herself, before she fell back into the wonder of the film.

Wednesday 19th August, 1946—'Highfields', Jeetho

Mrs Hughes posted the letter in the postbox outside the General Store and flopped into the driver's seat of the car. Mrs Hughes rarely flopped. "You know what, Coral? Life is short."

From Coral's vantage point, life was anything but short. She always had a list of chores to do, that took longer than all the hours in the day. Life seemed to drag on-and-on, not be as short as Mrs Hughes claimed.

"Let's treat ourselves to some shopping!"

Mrs Hughes was being frivolous. Mrs *'Be responsible and count-every-penny'* Hughes grabbed her basket and left Coral in the car. "Well, come on! Are you coming or not?"

Coral scrambled from the car and wondered if her life had taken on a weird dreamlike meaning. Like Fantasia. But in the Loch General Store.

"Those there," Mrs Hughes pointed to the shoes Mr Barker carefully dusted each morning, "I've seen you swooning over them, Coral. They are beautiful shiny patent shoes that any girl would love to own. Get them darling."

"Really?"

"Really. You have your own money. Enjoy it."

Mrs Hughes tried on dresses and easily dismissed the ones she didn't like. Her hands ran across the boldly coloured cardigans, and she perused the newly arrived silk stockings, not in a corner, but held them aloft so the ladies who had gathered to watch and mutter remarks to each other wouldn't miss a thing.

"A coat, my dear Coral. Which one have you always admired? The maize? Oh, it looks gorgeous on you! Don't forget some new gloves."

Coral smiled at the ladies gathered at the store's front steps. She heard something about *'not keeping a man'*, but they must be stupid. Mrs Hughes was married. Silly old gits.

When they arrived home, Coral helped Mrs Hughes bring in all their shopping, and made her a big pot of tea when she sat in her bedroom and cried most of the afternoon.

Goodbye Jeetho

'Highfields'
Jeetho
19th August, 1946.

Dear Mrs. Shaw,
I am writing direct to you to explain what has happened here recently.

My husband, on discharge from the R.A.A.F. was offered a very good position with the Soldier's Settlement Commission and after six months on the land he felt a bit discontented and accepted it.

We are so far unable to get vacant possession of our home in Camberwell, but expect to do so any day. In the meantime, my brother has let me one of his flats in East St. Kilda, but unfortunately there is only room for my husband, myself, and our older daughter who will meet us there.

Coral is anxious to come to our home in Camberwell when we can settle there, but in the meantime, it is not possible for me to accommodate her at the flat.

My younger son is staying on the farm with a married couple who will help with the work.

I expect to take possession of the flat on Saturday the 24th instance, but will probably not get a carrier until Monday, when I shall take Coral down and call in to see you to decide whether she will return to me when I make a home in Camberwell.

She has made some improvements, but is a girl who needs careful attention and rather strict discipline. Her mentality is low, and she is inclined to be very dirty, but I was feeling quite happy with the change for the better that I was able to see in her recently.

I should not like to see her go to a mistress who was lax in supervision.

You could ring me at the Loch exchange, or write to Jeetho if you have any plans I could help with.

Yours Sincerely,
Eileen Hughes

Mt. Evelyn
1946

Friday 23rd August, 1946—
C.W.D. Flinders Street Railway Building

John Oxford removed some papers from the briefcase he unceremoniously plonked on his desk. "Sorry to be late Mrs Shaw; I missed my tram this morning."

His superior was deep in thought and mumbled a response.

He organised his desk and gently dropped his briefcase into its usual resting spot behind his chair. "Given much thought to Mrs Hughes's letter?"

"There was a lady I interviewed recently..." Mrs Shaw sprang from her desk and started thumbing through the files in the cabinet. "She was desperate for help. Her husband and his employer asked whether we might have someone available. She has three young children, and her husband's often away."

"Has she filled in an application form?"

"Yes.... here it is!" Mrs Shaw stepped toward her desk while she read through her notes. "She hasn't had one of our girls before, but she needs help right now. Perhaps Coral can assist them in the meantime, and then go back to the Hughes family once they've settled."

"Sounds perfect."

Mrs Shaw picked up her pen and made a note across the bottom of Mrs Hughes's letter.

Coral to be placed with Mrs Dixon in Mt Evelyn until Mrs Hughes can accommodate her.

She leant back into her chair. "Mrs Hughes was perfect for her. We couldn't improve on that placement."

"Hopefully it will all be back to normal for her soon."

"Indeed, Mr Oxford."

Wednesday 28th August, 1946—
C.W.D. Flinders Street Railway Building

Children's Welfare Department

In accordance with arrangements, Coral will be placed with Mrs. Dixon in Mt Evelyn temporarily.
Date 29th August 1946
Wages 17/6 OP 2/6 per week.
Please send new wages book today please.

N.B. I would like to know the address of Mrs Hughes, where she is staying in St Kilda, please.
Signed,
Mrs. D. Shaw

Thursday 29th August, 1946—
Hereford Road, Mount Evelyn

The wind bustled through the car window and whipped Coral's hair all over her face. It wasn't like the wind at 'Highfields'. First, it wasn't as cold, and secondly and most importantly, she could control it. She wound the window up until the wind was gentler around her face.

Mrs Shaw looked into the back seat occasionally but other than that, probably forgot she was there. She said they were going to Mount Evelyn. *A mountain?* Sounded tall, Perhaps it had snow on the top, like the books she read at Mrs Hughes's. The little girl with plaits in her hair. *Heidi*, that was it.

When Mrs Reynold had come for her, she asked if Coral liked cake.

Mrs Hughes simply collected her once she was ready.

This time, she was sent. No choice, no decision, no information. Just sent.

"Almost there." Mrs Shaw kept her sing-song voice wherever she was.

Almost there?

There was only bush, and occasional puddles by the road from last night's rain.

No snow-peaked mountains, no crisp air, just bush and lots of it.

Little snippets of tin and wood splashed through the gaps in the trees. There were more houses than Jeetho here, tucked away through the bush, and no sign of any farms... yet.

The car chugged up a slope, rounded a hill, and Mrs Shaw slowed down, looking for a name among the dirt driveways. The city had numbers everywhere. They don't seem to use them in the country at all.

"Well, this is the right road; Hereford Road." Mrs Shaw came to a stop and checked her map and papers again. "It should be just ahead."

The driveway was skinny and bumpy and led to a clearing with a small house with a little verandah, some sheds, and an open paddock. No one came out to greet them. In fact, no one seemed to be home at all.

Coral stood still and held her suitcase in front of her, while Mrs Shaw did some surreptitious stickybeaking[1] around the house.

"Hello?" Mrs Shaw called.

Voices!

From the back of the house!

Mrs Shaw beckoned to Coral, and they rounded the house together along the side path. Water dripped on them as they passed under an overgrown bush that arched above them. Everything was damp, but it was colourful because of the dampness. It smelt funny, too. Not like the open winds of Highfields, or drifting farm smells, but of rich wet bush with lots of unfamiliar scents mingled with it.

The voice belonged to a stout woman who sat on the back porch on an old rickety chair. Her dark hair was in a tight bun, and her apron was dirty. Further down the block, two men worked at chopping wood. The older one chopped while the younger one gathered the wood into a wheelbarrow. They wore brown pants with braces over their dirty undershirts.

Three small children charged from the house and surrounded the woman and at the sight of their visitors became noisy and boisterous. They reminded Coral of her brothers and made her smile straight away.

Mrs Shaw stepped forward, "Mrs Dixon?"

---

1. Inquisitive prying

"Yep, that's me." The woman stood up and shook Mrs Shaw's gloved hand firmly and nodded into the yard. "My husband and his friend Walter are working on the firewood."

"I see," Mrs Shaw replied. "This is the girl you asked for. Her name is Coral Maxwell, and she's trained in general household duties, and I'm sure you'll find her a great help with the children."

Coral didn't hear the rest of the conversation; they talked about wages books and department visits while she made faces at the children. The children weren't shy at all and came to her immediately.

"Well then, I'll be off. You'll be all right, Coral?"

"Yes, Mrs Shaw."

Mrs Shaw had barely turned the corner to the side path when Mrs Dixon folded her arms and looked Coral up and down.

"So, what's your name again?"

"Coral, but I sign my name as Gladys because–"

"Haven't got time for crap, girl. You are who you are, and that's all there is to it. Take it from me. People tried to tell me who I should be, and I told them to drop dead. Drop dead, you hear me?"

"Yes, Mrs Dixon."

"How old are you?"

"Sixteen."

"Right. And what's your name then? Make up your mind."

Coral looked down at her shoes and squeezed the handle on her suitcase. "Coral."

"Right then, Coral, it seems you'll have to do." Mrs Dixon tilted her head to the back door. "Your room's on the right, off the kitchen. Put your suitcase in there and feed the children some lunch. There's some bread on the counter and jam in the larder."

The children followed her into the house and asked how long they'd have to wait for lunch. Coral didn't spend any time unpacking or admiring her room. There wasn't much to admire, really; a small dresser with wonky drawers, a simple bed and walls made of painted boards. "Come on then," she called to them, "Let's have some lunch."

Sunday 15th September, 1946—
Hereford Road, Mount Evelyn

Mrs Dixon didn't strike Coral as being as 'proper' as Mrs Hughes; she didn't correct her when she said the wrong word in a sentence, and she yelled quite a lot. She moved fast and barked orders, and the work always got done quick smart. Mrs Dixon didn't hum as she dusted, like Mrs Hughes did. She said humming annoyed her, so Coral hummed in her head, and when she got sick of humming, she made up stories from the serials in her magazines.

Coral always had time for the children, and they followed her around like little chickens until Mrs Dixon sent them outside to play.

"How are you meant to get your work done with those blighters around?" Mrs Dixon scooted the last of the littlies out the way.

"They'll be back at school before we know it."

"And not before time. You'll still have the little one under your feet, mind you."

Coral didn't mind at all. She preferred the children to Mrs Dixon any day.

Mrs Dixon also liked to drink and usually started with her after-lunch sherry, before graduating to scotch later in the afternoon.

That made Coral's afternoons perilous. Not in a scary kind of way, but just tense enough to keep her on her toes. Mrs Dixon's mood could develop in any direction during the afternoon, and Coral needed to be ready. She talked a lot about Walter when she was merry. Coral thought she'd talk more about her husband, but it seemed Walter was far more interesting. Coral gave up asking questions. She'd just get nonsense replies, anyway. A pleasant smile, a nod, or a laugh in the right place often kept Mrs Dixon satisfied and stopped her barking at Coral about some slight.

"Who do you want to be in the world, Coral?" she slurred. "Who they tell you to be? Now's the time to start thinking, girl. You decide your fate, not them and not any man! Not even the department."

"Mrs Shaw has always been nice to me."

"Of course she has, you silly girl. That's what they pay her to do."

Walter must've been someone very special. It seemed everyone in the household fought about him. Even when Mr. Dixon came home from the city, the couple fought a lot and Walter's name always ended up in the mix. When it got too loud, Coral would take the children and hide in her room and read them stories from her magazines. When they read all of them, Coral would make up her own, by mixing the stories she'd read together into new ones.

"Will you get some new stories for us?" the children asked.

"Next time I get paid. I promise."

Saturday 5th October, 1946—
Hereford Road, Mount Evelyn

Coral flipped open the wages book and signed her name neatly next to the amount of 15 shillings. The rest of the page was blank. "Aren't you supposed to record what I spend my money on?"

Mrs Dixon rested on the couch with her feet up on a stool. Her pregnant belly was just beginning to show. "Wish this Bex would start working," she moaned. "What was that?"

"You're meant to record what I spend my money on."

"Why?"

"That's what Mrs Hughes did."

"For God's sake, Coral, the department doesn't even know we're not married," she laughed. "You don't want them to know *everything* about you, do you?"

Did she? Coral didn't know anymore. "I'm off to the store."

"To get more of those magazines, I bet. Tell you what, Coral, if I see you reading instead of working again, I'll burn the whole bloody lot."

"Yes, Mrs Dixon."

Coral took Hereford Road, down to York Road, and into Station Street. She knew about the shortcut through the back, but this way she'd be out of the house that little bit longer, and the walk was always enjoyable. She missed seeing the train go by but heard its whistle from inside the store.

The shopkeeper had a big bulbous nose and white hair that grew on the tops of his ears. Coral always tried hard not to stare, but they went off on odd angles like grasshopper legs. When she entered, he was bagging flour for a customer. The shopkeeper didn't know her name, but he was always kind to her. Once he'd even given her some tea from out the back when she'd panicked about not having any to take back to Mrs Dixon; Coral was convinced he'd shared from his very own caddy.

She knew his name because of two things. His nametag said Mervin Cole, and Mrs Dixon would sing 'old dud Cole was a boring old soul'.

Coral made her selection and approached the counter. Mr Cole wore a grin that made his cheeks go even rounder. "I thought you'd be in early for this one. I don't suppose that cover interests you much, though."

There was some cricketer on the cover, and Coral didn't care much for cricket.

"That's Wally Hammond, England's test captain." Mr Cole pretended to fend off a ball with an imaginary cricket bat. "But it's all about those stories for you, isn't it?"

Coral smiled and handed him three-pence.

"What? No sweeties today?"

"Not today, thank you. But I'll see you for next week's copy."

"Good-o, we'll see you then."

Christmas Eve, 1946—
Hereford Road, Mount Evelyn

Coral tip toed through the back door and checked on the sleeping children before moving to the lounge room. The music and hymns from the carol by candlelight service still sang in her head. She remembered to stop humming the moment she saw Mrs Dixon stirring on the lounge.

"Cup of tea, Mrs Dixon?"

Mrs Dixon held up her sherry glass. "Another of these would be in good order. After all, it's Christmas, isn't it?"

Coral poured Mrs Dixon her sherry and made herself a cup of tea.

"They said there were about a thousand people at the carols tonight."

"A thousand? Well, that's a good turnout. Given the heat."

"I'm glad the cool change came through early. It would've been awful with all those people in the heat."

"They kept it at the Recreation Reserve? They might've moved it if it rained."

"It was lovely. Reverend Thomas stood on the back of a truck so everyone could see him, and there were so many candles, it was easy enough to read the words in the programme. At the end, they said they'd raised £18."

Mrs Dixon had a strange frown on her face. "£18! Who's getting that?"

"It's for the kindergarten."

"That'd be right."

Sunday 12th January, 1947—
Hereford Road, Mount Evelyn

"Coral!!!"

Mrs Dixon was angry, but it was only morning, so it couldn't be the sherry or the scotch. Coral stopped pegging clothes on the line and ran inside and found Mrs Dixon in her bedroom.

"For God's sake, Coral, stop pissing in my beds. Anyone'd think you were younger than these kids. Look what you've done to my mattress! Don't think I won't be complaining to the department. They can buy me a new mattress, sending me a girl who ruins my things! You're not much of a helper, are you?"

"Sorry Mrs Dixon. I'll try bett—"

"Just get away from me. Get back to the line."

'Pregnant Mrs Dixon' didn't quite carry herself the same way as other pregnant women Coral had seen. To be honest, she hadn't seen that many at all; some in the Loch General Store, others being helped from cars and trucks when they shopped. They also seemed so dainty and everyone was protective of them; as if they were extra special. Everyone in Jeetho celebrated when a birth was announced. Coral didn't even know the people's names, but it was nice to bask in all the warmth of good wishes to the new family, and even the men toasted the child whenever they got the chance.

Coral decided Mrs Dixon was a different kind of pregnant. Maybe it was the babies who made the mothers act differently; as if angry babies made the mothers angry, and the other women she'd seen were having quiet and demure babies.

Who knew? Coral just knew she'd better get a move on with her chores and stay out of Mrs Dixon's way today. She jumped when Mrs Dixon appeared beside her.

"Once you've done your chores, go and post this letter. Take the kids for a walk."

"Yes, Mrs Dixon." Coral slipped the envelope into her apron pocket. She expected the letter was just like the others. She tried not to look at who it was addressed to but couldn't help herself. Once Mrs Dixon had stepped inside the house, she pulled it from the pocket. There it was, neatly addressed on the front of the envelope.

'Mr Walter A. Ellis.'

Wednesday 5th February, 1947—
C.W.D. Flinders Street Railway Building

SERVICE REPORT/DEPARTMENT VISIT

Home suitable–yes.

Room in house, comfortably furnished.

Helps generally. Mrs Dixon has 3 young children. Girl works from 7.30am–6.30pm with free time in the afternoon.

Coral says she is happy in the home and loves the children.

Does not attend church although it's within walking distance and she's advised to go.

Mrs. Dixon does not give a good report, although she is thankful to have any help at all.

Other information - This girl is a bed wetter although improved in this respect with Mrs. Hughes. Mrs Dixon did not discover this weakness until Coral had been with her a month. Consequently, bed mattress was ruined.

Also, Mrs Dixon said Coral will stop in the middle of any task to read a book or paper. I saw the girl myself down the street, looking rather down at heel, leaning up against a shop window and reading the Women's Mirror which she had just purchased.

Thursday 20th February, 1947—Hereford Road, Mount Evelyn

"It's a boy!"

The midwife's head poked out of Mrs Dixon's bedroom, delivered the news, and then disappeared back inside. Coral went to tell the children who'd been ordered to play outside.

"A little brother; how exciting for you."

The children seemed happy, but the eldest, Tommy, said "Pity Dad isn't here."

"It *is* a pity, but he's working hard for you all. Remember that."

Mrs Dixon rested in bed while Coral took care of the household.

"Coral," she'd call. "Take the baby. I just feel I need to rest a little more."

Coral didn't mind at all. Her favourite part of the day was when Mrs Dixon was sound asleep, and she could rock baby John off to sleep in her arms. She hated putting him down to 'cry it out'.

"It's good for their lungs," Mrs Dixon told her, but she still loved carrying him around with her, snuggled close and peaceful.

Coral rushed to get one of her magazines and looked up a poem she read about the days of the week and babies. She found it on page 14.

Monday's child is fair of face,
Tuesday's child is full of grace.
Wednesday's child is full of woe,
Thursday's child has far to go...

She watched John pull funny faces as he slept. "Far to go hey?" she whispered. "Wonder what your little life will be like? It's all brand new, not a mark or stain on you. You could become anything!"

She wondered what day of the week she was born, and if there was anyone who could tell her that.

<u>Saturday 12th April, 1947—</u>
<u>Hereford Road, Mount Evelyn</u>

With a heavy heart, Coral realised babies don't always bring peace to households, and life could return to 'normal' quicker than you might think.

At first it was just the tension in the air, or the way Mr Dixon snapped when he came home. Sometimes it was the way Mrs Dixon strutted through the house and smirked at him, but Coral sensed when a storm of the Dixon kind was brewing.

She usually had time to gather the children into her room, to read stories and snuggle while the tempest raged on the other side of the door, but this time was a little different.

Walter had a 'falling out' with his people and had recently come to stay at the Dixon home.

But when Mr Dixon got home and was told the news, he wasn't happy about it at all.

Coral and the children stayed under the covers of her bed and sang quiet songs, while the sounds of fists meeting flesh pushed their way through the walls. All three of them were at it this time! Amid the smashing plates, shouting, and stomping around, Coral told stories of brave princes, gentle princesses and dragons that were always overcome by goodness and a powerful sword.

At one stage, Coral heard Mr Dixon yelling about a letter.

Her voice squeaked as she watched the handle of her door for any movement.

Thankfully, none came *this* time.

Monday 30th June, 1947— Hereford Road, Mount Evelyn

Coral stopped dusting the china cabinet and scratched at her cheek. "There's a truck in the driveway, Mrs Dixon." It was a flatbed delivery truck, like the one the greengrocer used, but Coral hadn't seen this one around before.

"Right on time." Mrs Dixon brushed past her in a flurry. "Come along then child, we're moving."

"Moving? Where?"

The children, bellies full of Weetbix, and limbs full of energy ran to the truck and fired off scores of questions that Coral couldn't answer. It was hard enough to round them up, let alone set to packing the house.

"Nobody touch my china," Mrs Dixon called, "I'll do that."

Coral's body felt 10lbs lighter. The last thing she wanted to do was be cursed at every time she handled a plate the wrong way.

It took most of the day to bundle, pack, shove and tie the Dixon's belongings to the truck. The dining chairs hung along the outside in such a way it created a fence that helped hold their other items in place. They were sure to leave a hollow in the middle of the packing which they filled with blankets and clothing. Coral and the children settled there like nestlings, wearing heavy coats and blankets against the cold winter air. Coral was relieved Mrs Dixon chose to keep baby John in the truck with her.

It was a long cold drive, and if anyone had bothered to ask Coral, she would've told them she was miserable, but the children thought it was jolly good fun. She tried to be light-hearted along with them, but was terrified they'd fall from the truck, or something would topple and crush them at every turn. Rainclouds chased them the entire way. The little ones already had sniffles, and the wind kept blowing little Mary's hair into her snot. Coral was out of gratitude not long after she was out of handkerchiefs.

The truck pulled up outside a small house on a dirt road. It was farming country, but not green like Jeetho. Flat and dry. A funny faded yellow colour.

Without the wind to compete with, Mrs Dixon's voice rang clear into their nest. "Home Sweet Home."

Coral craned her neck but couldn't see much more than before. "Where are we?"

"Mernda."

Wednesday 30th July, 1947—
C.W.D. Flinders Street Railway Building

Mrs Shaw sat with a plop into her chair and rested her head in her hands. She hadn't bothered to remove her coat and her hat tilted unceremoniously to one side.

Mr Oxford waited for her explanation as to her dishevelment, knowing she had been conducting department visits that morning, but she didn't offer one at all.

"My dear Mrs Shaw, whatever is the matter?"

"I..." she began, but words failed her. Instead, she handed Mr Oxford her hand-written notes from the morning.

Coral MAXWELL (66420) Department Visit 30.07.47

On calling at the above address today, I learned that Mrs Dixon had moved the family to Mernda a month ago. Home said to be one mile from the Railway Station.

From information received of a confidential nature, I learned that employer does not hold a good name. She is often seen in hotels and under the influence of alcohol. She has also associated very intimately with a young man named Walter Ellis.

I called on Mrs. Ellis to see what she knew of Mrs. Dixon. She was very distressed about such a friendship and said they had been most unhappy over such an affair.

Husband of employer is a car driver, employed in Melbourne. He was to go home each weekend, but has not been doing so over recent months.

Employer has not made any savings deposits since girl was placed with her almost a year ago.

Could this girl be transferred to another position at an early date as such an environment would not be helpful.

Notes—Girl to be transferred to other employment. Employer will be informed that inspector will call on the 7th prox.

This position was only a temporary one. Mrs Hughes, former employer has said she would take girl back, but she has not made any further representation to this department regarding same.

"Oh, good Lord," John Oxford slumped into his seat. "Where *is* she?" Mrs Shaw shrugged. "I don't know. I'm not waiting for the Inspector though, John, I'm driving out to Mernda myself."

Friday 1st August, 1947—
C.W.D. Flinders Street Railway Building

Mr Oxford held his hat against the bitter wind in Flinders Street and helped Mrs Shaw into the car. She wound the window down far enough to give him instructions. "Be sure to post that bill to Mrs Dixon today. She hasn't sent any money for Coral in 48 weeks."

"Will do." Mr Oxford tapped the car's roof and Dulcie Shaw was on her way to Mernda.

Friday 1st August, 1947—Mernda

"Time to go now, Coral," Mrs Shaw stepped toward the front door, her heart beating hard. She was so close to getting her out of Mrs Dixon's home.

It hadn't taken her much of the morning to find the Dixon's home. Mernda wasn't heavily populated and a quick check in at the General Store and Publican House gave her solid directions.

Coral knelt next to the children and gave them each a hug goodbye. The pillowcase containing her belongings sat like a lump beside them.

"On ya way then, hopeless girl," Mrs Dixon leant against her china cabinet and Dulcie Shaw bit her lip so as not to cause any further offence.

Coral didn't care so much. Mrs Dixon was always angry with everyone; her husband, Walter, the landlord, Mrs Shaw, so it didn't really matter that she was angry at her too.

"Come now, Coral, gather your things. Where are your shoes?"

"I don't have any."

"No shoes? Why in the blazes—"

"Here, take these." Mrs Dixon flicked her slippers at Coral. "They're too big for my feet, anyway."

Mrs Shaw didn't hide her eye roll and turned Coral toward the waiting car.

The car bumped its way through the spooned gutter, down a lane surrounded by paddocks and turned into Epping Road. Mrs Shaw alternated between sighing and frowning while Coral looked out the window and wondered who was going to make dinner for the children that night. Bet Mrs Dixon won't keep reading that story to them either.

"Oh dear Coral," Mrs Shaw said, "Placements aren't meant to be like that. Are you alright?"

Coral shrugged. "Mrs Hughes's home was much nicer."

"I bet it was."

"How were you all surviving out there?"

"Mrs Dixon said the whole family had to pitch in and help. And to do whatever we could to get rabbits or food. Sometimes we swapped rabbits for vegetables. Other times men came with food and meat, and…"

"And?" Mrs Shaw's throat tightened.

"And I was a good girl. Mrs Dixon says that making sure we have firewood to keep us warm is an altogether higher form of good than most people realise."

Mrs Shaw's heart sank to her stomach. "I see."

"Mrs Dixon says she keeps them happy to make sure we eat. We all have to do stuff we don't like. Sometimes with people we don't like. But it's okay, really. We got rabbits and firewood and once even some beef."

"You stayed a good girl though, didn't you, Coral?"

"Sometimes you don't get to choose those things, do you? Mrs Dixon said she's never gone hungry."

"I see."

"Can I wind the window down?"

"Of course. Are you feeling alright?"

"Just a bit sick. Haven't been in a car for a while."

"Well, I need to find some petrol and to make a phone call. The stop and fresh air might do you good."

Coral nodded and watched the bush and the paddocks pass by in a blur.

Ding! Ding!

The bell rang as Mrs Shaw's car pulled into the service station and a man appeared at her side. "Fill 'er up?"

"Yes please. Oh, public phone?"

"Inside."

Coral found the magazine stand quicker than Mrs Shaw found the phone. "Wait here Coral, I'll be back soon."

Coral nodded but didn't really hear. The new *Women's Weekly* was out!

Mrs Shaw plucked at the lint on her coat while she waited for the operator to connect her call.

Goodbye Mt. Evelyn

Friday 1st August, 1947—
C.W.D. Flinders Street Railway Building

The phone in the office rang, and John Oxford leapt for it from the other side of the desk. "Oxford."

"John, it's Dulcie,"

"Did you get Coral without any problems?"

"Almost. I'm calling from the general store in Wollert."

"Still a long way out, then."

"I've had some conversations with Coral that have left me terribly concerned."

"Oh?"

"We need to put her somewhere quiet for a while. Where she can rest, recuperate, and be under a watchful eye. She's seen enough." Dulcie groaned and tears pricked her eyes. "How do we expect to raise children when the adults can be horrendous and give no thought to the souls in their care?"

"It's that bad?"

"I'm hoping not, but nothing surprises me anymore."

"It's not like you to be so cynical, Mrs Shaw."

"It's been a long day, Mr Oxford."

Mr Oxford rifled through a filing cabinet. "What about Matron Flagg? She's always been a stalwart for the correct and proper training of home girls. She's now at…… let me see, Spring House, in the city."

"Then she'll be in need of extra hands."

"I'll call her, tell her to expect you, and get a service agreement sent over to her today."

"I'm worried about this child, John. And she's still is very much a child."

"She'll soon be under Matron Flagg's watchful eye."

"Can't think of anything better for her. I'll come into the office after I drop her off."

"See you then."

Mrs Shaw replaced the receiver and watched the gangly girl with the too big slippers flip through the magazine pages.

The attendant shook his head at Coral as he entered and met Mrs Shaw at the counter.

"That'll be 1 pound, 8 shillings thanks."

Mrs Shaw glanced back at Coral, "We'll take that magazine too."

Coral's mouth dropped open, "Really Mrs Shaw? Thank you!"

Spring House
1947

Friday 1st August, 1947—
'Spring House', Spring Street, Melbourne

Coral clutched the magazine in her hand and slid into the backseat of Mrs Shaw's car. Somehow, she felt less alone when she had her stories, even in a tiny place called Wollert. For a moment, she wondered where she might be going, but it didn't matter, anyway. It's easy to lose interest in your life when you have no say in it.

'Spring House.'
That's what the sign above the entrance on the white building said. It sounded like a nice place. Spring was always pretty, and all those iron lace balconies gave it a romantic feel. Ohh, it's on *Spring* Street. Suddenly, it wasn't a feeling anymore; it was just a place. Coral lifted her chin all the way back. A four-storey place!

To Coral's surprise, Mrs Shaw didn't knock on the door but strolled straight inside. A lady with an apron approached them and Mrs Shaw spoke first.

"Mrs Shaw from the Welfare Department to see Matron Flagg, please."

"Of course," the lady replied, "You can wait here in the resident's lounge."

The lounge was light and bright. Two girls in banking uniforms chatted on one of the couches, and the large mantle boasted a handsome radio. Coral smiled at the bookcase, so filled with books some lay on their sides. The lamp in the corner had a crooked lampshade, and Coral's hands itched to straighten it.

"Ah Mrs Shaw, pleased to see you again."

"Matron Flagg, this is Coral Maxwell."

The matron stood tall and wide. Well, her shoulders were wide, the rest of her was 'normal' size, but she was still very tall, and very serious. She frowned the way Mrs Dixon did when she saw a bug on the floor. Coral assumed, as usual, that she was the bug in question.

Mrs Shaw cupped Coral's elbow. "You'll feel right at home here. Matron Flagg was at The Catherine Booth Home; but not while you were there. She knows all about life for our girls in care and often speaks and participates in public forums about this very subject."

Coral didn't remember her, of course, but she knew the name and the cane she often inflicted on the girls. She stretched a polite smile across her lips.

The matron deferred to Mrs Shaw. "Oh, thank you, Mrs Shaw. You are too kind. I do try to do my best, with the help of our good Lord, of course."

"Of course, Matron."

Two girls passed by with books in their arms and Coral's eyes followed them down the hallway. They must be studying. They could be anything they want to be. "So, I'll be living here?"

"Yes, but not as one of the residents," Matron Flagg said, "Spring House is a hostel. It's a home away from home for young ladies who are studying or working in the city."

Mrs Shaw patted Coral's arm. "You'll be in service to the Matron."

"Oh, I see. Alright."

Matron Flagg gestured to a small table in the corner of the resident's lounge. "Mr Oxford kindly sent the service agreement papers over by courier and they're signed and ready for you."

Mrs Shaw flipped through the pages one-by-one. "Coral, your wages are up to 25 shillings, and Matron will still send your two shillings and sixpence to our office to add to your savings account."

Coral smiled and nodded. *25 shillings*. It's like everything was new again, and everything that happened before this day didn't matter.

She was sick of thinking about Mrs Dixon and keeping her happy, and she looking forward to having money again. Mrs Dixon stopped paying her wages months ago, told her to be grateful for what she had, and then blamed her for everything that went wrong or cost them money. Coral hated being blamed for stuff; just the thought of it made her flush and her tummy twist hard. She didn't want to be Coral anymore. A new start meant new choices; what to do with her 25 shillings, and what name to use.

"Be good now Coral, do what Matron tells you."

"Yes, Mrs Shaw."

The door closed behind Mrs Shaw with a soft thud.

"This way Coral." Matron led the way with Coral and her pillowcase and too big slippers following behind. "This will be your room."

It was a small room on the second floor. At first, Coral wasn't even sure it was a bedroom. It had a slanty roof and just enough room for a bed pushed up under the slanty side. When she sat on the bed, she had to lean forward so as not to hit her head. There was a small sash window that looked out onto a brick wall, and an old dresser with drawers that jammed when you slid them in and out, so you had to kind of walk them in, wiggling one side and then the other.

It smelt like floor cleaner; it might have been a storage cupboard once. But for now, it was home.

"You can leave your bag here. I'll show you to the kitchen and you can get to work."

Coral plopped her pillowcase on the bed. "Yes, Matron."

Friday 1st August, 1947—
C.W.D. Flinders Street Railway Building

By the time Dulcie Shaw reached the office, it was dark, John had gone home, and she was exhausted.

She rode the elevator and walked up the long hallway but stepped into a different office than her own. She dropped her notes on the middle of the Inspector's desk.

'As directed by Mr Devine, I removed Coral MAXWELL (66420) from the home of Mrs Dixon.

Girl looked well nourished, and also the four small children in the home.

Coral did not have a pair of wearable shoes. Mrs Dixon lent her a pair to come down in.

From what I could learn, mostly from Coral's remarks, there is no money coming in to the home. Mr Dixon was out rabbiting. They have lived on rabbits for weeks. Coral said the butcher did not call lately, and they have an eviction order against them.

Mr Dixon had sold his car and will not work.

Mr Dixon's employer, and who previously recommended this family has been up to Mernda and offered to buy him another car and give him work.

I mentioned the facts leading up to the removal of the girl.

Employer said "Why, Walter is just a boy, a friend of my husband's." I replied, "Yes, I know. He was helping with the wood the day I took Coral along to you."

She said she had not been in hotels, other than with her husband.

Regarding Coral's savings and the balance of her wages, employer said "Henry would send a cheque." Shoes purchased from Coral's savings.'

Friday 15th August, 1947—
'Spring House', Spring Street, Melbourne

The ground floor of Spring House contained the kitchen, dining room, and resident's lounge. The resident's rooms filled each storey after that, each floor with its own bathroom and toilet. But Coral loved the rooftop garden the most. It was quiet up there at night, well, not truly quiet like in the country; there were always people in the streets making noise. Coral enjoyed wondering where they were headed. The city was so big it could be anywhere. One night, a group of girls laughed so loudly as they passed under her gaze she imagined Matron Flagg at the window, tutting at them as they walked past. *'Revellers',* she'd mutter.

But even from up there, she could spot the bright yellow dot of dandelions under the streetlights. They were probably as confused as her, opening at the streetlights instead of the sun. Coral smiled at the lights and closed her eyes against a breeze that bustled along the street and whipped up the face of the building. She was in the city again. No more fields and trees as far as the eye could see. Just the sounds of her childhood. Rumbling trams and busy streets, and not a bloody rabbit in sight.

The staff's rooms were nicer than Coral's; she'd seen inside them while vacuuming the hallway. It made sense the residents had pleasant rooms, after all, the girls were studying or working in offices in the city and paid for their rooms. Coral seemed stuck in the middle, not quite a staff member with some level of respect, but not a resident with lovely clothes and a job either. It seemed fitting really, a funny odd shaped room, for a funny odd shaped girl.

She dreamed of wearing a sweet little bolero jacket, and twirling around in a floral dress, but instead she wore a plain green dress with a belt tied around the middle of her too big waist. The girls in her magazines didn't have a waist like hers, so she liked to keep it hidden and was secretly thankful her apron covered her dress most of the time. If she couldn't see the green dress, she could imagine she had a pretty floral dress on underneath.

"Coral!" Matron Flagg called her from her office near the kitchen and Coral already knew to hasten to her call. "Here are your wages, dear. Now be wise with it."

"Thank you, Matron." The wages book was blank other than one word - *wages*. Looked like Mrs Hughes was the only one who was a stickler for the rules after all.

Matron tapped her finger on the wages book. "Why are you signing your name as Gladys?"

"Because I want to."

"But your name is Coral."

"I know that, Matron."

Matron Flagg frowned, pulled her head back a little, and shook it. By then, Coral was already at the front door. "Where are you off to in such a hurry?"

"Matinee at the pictures! Can't be late!"

"Oh, for God's sake Coral!" This time it was Coral berating herself and stripping the bed. At least she knew where to find new sheets and adds the old ones to the laundry hamper before anyone else was up.

She stood back and admired her newly made bed. "There, all done." The bedspread with the orange flowers looked nice in the shadow of her little slanty ceiling. Coral gasped, "Not yet, it's not!" She grabbed at the magazines on the floor and stuffed them under her mattress and hid her books inside the dresser. One lecture from Matron Flagg about literature being a bad influence on young people was all it took for Coral to keep all her treasure hidden. She still couldn't quite believe that people came from far and wide to hear Matron Flagg's thoughts on the evils of literature, and how hostels were going to be the great new reformation of institutionalised girls and boys. Matron Flagg said that was four years ago now, and she was certainly proud of Spring House. But wherever Coral looked, she couldn't see where homies like her fit into the matron's grand plan.

INSPECTOR'S REPORT
Monday 13th October, 1947—
C.W.D. Flinders Street Railway Building

SERVICE REPORT
Suitable home.
Room to herself. Accommodation not all together satisfactory for staff.
Helping in the kitchen at present time, is on the relieving staff 8 hrs.
Employer satisfied.
Healthy, mentally slow suffers enuresis but is improving.
Attends church.
    Other notes–Coral is not a particularly clean girl and is not at all trim in her appearance. She is going to try to improve herself. Miss Flagg is giving good supervision; girl is saving her money. Has been unwell, but Matron Flagg assures it is nothing to be concerned about.

Friday 14th November, 1947—
'Spring House', Spring Street, Melbourne

The roast lamb was in the oven, and the kitchen staff worked on the side dishes.

"How many times have I got to...?" Julia slapped at Coral's hand. "Stop picking girl."

Coral laughed at Julia's stern look and continued peeling the carrots. She was more like a mother than the head of the kitchen and the peas she shelled were irresistible. More like sweeties than vegetables.

Coral started on some new carrots and suddenly felt sick. Maybe it was the peas. Julia was right; she'd get sick if she kept picking before dinnertime. But it wasn't just before dinnertime. Coral snacked after breakfast and before lunch too, sometimes after lunch as well. She'd once taken a few slices of fruit cake meant for the residents and hidden them under her bed with the magazines.

She was so embarrassed that she tried a new diet she read about in the Woman's Mirror. She only managed to stay with it for two days. What was the point when her dress still didn't fit, and Julia still accused her of taking food?

The residents went off to work in their offices dressed in belted dresses and tight skirts, and Coral bemoaned the fact that if she tied her apron tighter it only made her look fatter.

"One ticket to *Sinbad the Sailor*, please." Coral adored the pictures. It wasn't the same as reading where she had to make up the pictures in her head. The movies meant she got to live in someone else's imagination for a while. While she was in that theatre seat, she wasn't a chubby homie who still wet the bed; she could be anyone. That day, she was a sailor! Last week, she was Loretta Young, a farmer's daughter, and before that she was Esther Williams and part of a bull fighting family! Coral sighed when the lights came back on, but there was always a new show to look forward to next week.

Thursday 25th December, 1947— 'Spring House', Spring Street, Melbourne

"Merry Christmas, Matron."

"Merry Christmas, Coral."

Spring House was quieter than usual. Most of the girls had families to return to for Christmas, or friends who invited them out of the city for Christmas lunch. Coral didn't mind spending the day with Matron Flagg. The service at the citadel was nice, and she loved hearing the church bells ring out across the city.

Matron Flagg pulled her coat collar up against the cold. "Can you believe this day? It's supposed to be summer. Let's get home."

Coral hurried home alongside her, not so much to get out of the cold, but to get home to their special treat. They were having a roast chicken for Christmas Day.

"What fine potatoes Coral."

"Thank you, Matron." Coral made a dive for the parson's nose. She'd spent a year imagining this moment!

"Parson's nose, eh? Never liked it myself, so it's all yours." Matron Flagg helped herself to a leg and added pumpkin and peas to her plate. "How did the carols go last night?"

Coral chewed quickly and swallowed a lump of potato before it was ready. "It was wonderful Matron. All those lights in Alexandra Park, and lovely singing. But you know what they did?" Coral didn't give Matron Flagg a chance to answer. "They used a short-wave radio to contact the Australian soldiers in Japan. They sang 'Silent Night' to us! Isn't that fascinating?"

"It truly is a marvel, what we're capable of these days. And the rain?"

"You'd never believe it. We thought they'd cancel the festival, but it stopped raining just as it began, and guess what?"

Matron Flagg had just bitten into one of Coral's crispy potatoes and raised her eyebrows in response.

"It started again as soon as it was finished!"

"It's been a very strange Christmas for us, hasn't it? I was chatting with Mavis at the Citadel and her brother in Hotham phoned to say it was snowing there. Fancy that! A white Christmas in Australia!"

"It seems the world is turning on its head."

"That it does."

Coral collected the empty plates and made her way to the kitchen. She was absolutely stuffed.

Matron called to her from the dining room, "If you don't mind, I'm not feeling terribly like pudding right now. We could always have it when I return this afternoon."

That sounded perfect to Coral. "Yes, when you're back from visiting with your people, we'll have a cup of tea and some pudding." Her body relaxed at not having to shove more food into it.

Matron Flagg pinned her hat in place, using the mirror in the foyer. "Here," she said to Coral and took a box from her bag, "Merry Christmas."

Coral opened the little brown paper package and found two metal hair slides inside. "Thank you, Matron, they're beautiful and I'll wear them every day. Oh, and before you go..." Coral ran to her room and unearthed a small box wrapped in a shop's gift paper. "This is for you. Merry Christmas."

Matron opened her small box of chocolates, declared them very special, and tucked them inside her handbag. "Are you sure you won't join me?"

"No thanks. I'm still tired from last night."

"Very well."

<u>Monday 15th March, 1948—</u>
<u>'Spring House', Spring Street, Melbourne</u>

"Oh, how could you, Coral? How could you? Bringing such shame upon us!"

Coral's eyes stretched open. Was Matron shouting at her? She *did* say 'Coral', but Coral was just standing there doing nothing. She'd only stretched her back because it hurt. How was folding sheets shameful? Matron Flagg yelled while Coral stood with her mouth open. Coral's lack of response infuriated the matron further; her face became redder by the second

Julia was nearby and rushed to the disturbance. She arrived just as Matron covered Coral with one of the sheets. "Get the nurse. Oh, get the nurse!"

Coral stared at the matron. Goodness! *The Nurse.* What was wrong? She woke up with a small headache that morning, but nothing else was different. This time her feet had trouble keeping up with the matron's as she was bundled, sheet and all, into the nurse's office.

The nurse had a little office on the ground floor. She was there chiefly for the residents in case of accidents and unforeseen circumstances and had broad knowledge in all things medical. Coral had only ever said hello to the nurse before. Her name was Jane, and she always had a smile ready for her. That thought comforted Coral, although she didn't know why.

"Just... just lie down!" Matron Flagg gestured to the bed that served as an examination table.

When she turned back to the door, the nurse scurried into the room. "Whatever is going on? They just called me to—"

"Outside!" Matron Flagg steered the nurse outside the door, and they talked in muffled exclamations. It was serious... whatever it was.

Jane smiled her usual smile when she entered the room, followed closely by Matron Flagg, who was still red in the face.

Jane patted Coral's shoulder. "I just need to feel your tummy for a little bit. Will that be alright?"

Jane felt all around Coral's tummy, sometimes gently, sometimes quite firmly, and then pulled a tape measure from her pocket. She measured from her underpants to her breastbone, then nodded at Matron Flagg. "Seven months I'd say."

"Seven Months!" Matron Flagg's face went redder than before and spittle formed in the corners of her mouth, "I must make a phone call. Coral, go back to your room and wait there."

The matron stormed out of the room, and Jane helped Coral to her feet.

"Seven months of what?" she whispered to Jane.

"Let's see dear. Seven months pregnant, which means you'll be having your baby in about two months."

"A baby? Me?"

"Yes, and in only two months."

"You deceptive little whore!" Matron Flagg barged into Coral's room with nary a knock. "You hid this from me all along. How did this happen?"

"I don't know."

"What do you mean, you don't know, you stupid girl? Who have you been with?"

Coral's voice was shaky. "Been with?"

"Yes,"

She must mean the pictures. "Umm,... the girls from here; sometimes with friends."

"No, what men have you been with?"

The way she said *'been with'* was weird. Did she mean...

"Physically, with your underclothes removed."

Oh, that kind of been with. Matron's face was still red. No one told Coral she wasn't supposed to do that. The Home said nothing; the men certainly didn't.

She didn't know it was bad.

That she was bad.

But Matron Flagg made sure she knew it now.

Monday 15th March, 1948—
C.W.D. Flinders Street Railway Buildings

The phone rang just as Mr Oxford downed the last of his cup of tea. "Oxford." It was the way he always answered his extension, so Janet knew she'd placed the call correctly.

This time there was no Janet, just Matron Flagg at full volume.

"Your girl is pregnant!"

"What girl is what?"

"Coral. She's seven months pregnant and bringing shame on Spring House. She must be gone now. Just imagine what it looks like!"

"Seven months? Did you not—"

"She's a slovenly girl, Mr Oxford. She has an unshapely figure and her behaviour didn't warrant any reprimands. But that's beside the point. I want her out of Spring House now!"

"Have you taken a statement from the girl?"

"She claims not to know anything. And a liar too."

"Please contact the police to take a report, Matron Flagg."

"Certainly. Not that it would do any good. She should have known better."

"Matron Flagg!" John Oxford yelled into the receiver. He had one brief moment to control his outburst, but he let it slide from his reach. She needed to know some truths. "Matron Flagg, how is she to *know better* when there is no one to teach her these things? Don't forget, we send these girls out into the world with no social education. We decide that is a parent's task, and then we fail these girls by not acting as parents. There are men that *prey* on these girls; on their vulnerability and naivete. Forgive me Matron Flagg, but don't tell me she should've known better. The entire point is that she didn't, and that is through no fault of her own." John Oxford listened for a response but didn't receive one. "Good day Matron Flagg."

Matron Flagg replaced the receiver without a word.

Goodbye Spring House

Wednesday 17th March, 1948—
C.W.D. Flinders Street Railway Building

Contacted Sister Rosalind Kelly, City Mission, Albion St., East Brunswick, regarding the girl's admission to their maternity home. Sister states Coral Maxwell would be admitted immediately.

Mr Oxford leant back in his chair waved a piece of paper above his head. "Looks like we've found a placement for Coral at the City Mission Maternity Home."

Mrs Shaw was impressed. "That was quick work."

"Thank goodness. Look, I know Matron Flagg wants her out of Spring House as soon as possible, but I think I want her out of there more than she does. Any other news?"

"Yep, I've just read the basic report. Coral said that since being employed at Spring House, she attended picture shows and Salvation Army meetings with other employees as arranged by Matron Flagg. She visited friends in Burnley, and occasionally she went to the pictures alone. One night, a few months ago, a young man who said his name was John spoke to her. They walked up to the gardens near Spring House, and misconduct took place. He left her to find her way home alone."

Mr Oxford shook his head and sighed as Mrs Shaw continued.

"She said she accidentally met him three or four weeks later. On this occasion, they went to another garden and the same behaviour occurred. Coral has never seen him since. She does not know his surname, nor his address."

"According to Matron Flagg, she's showing much evidence of approaching motherhood."

"There's something not right here, Mr Oxford."

"What do you mean?"

"Coral's only been at Spring House for seven months."

Mr Oxford gathered their empty teacups and prepared to leave the office. "Perhaps you can remind Matron Flagg of that when you call to let her know Coral is to be transferred on the 19th. I'm sure you'll make her day."

Friday 19th March, 1948—
C.W.D. Flinders Street Railway Building

Girl admitted to City Mission Maternity Home today.

City Mission
1948

Friday 19th March, 1948—
City Mission Maternity Home, Albion Street, East Brunswick

The grand old house looked out of place among the regular houses on their regular blocks. It was a strange-looking building, with a large chimney running straight up the centre, and a lovely little portico over the front door.

"Watch your step." The driver held the car door open; just like they did in Jeetho for expectant mothers. Coral carefully stretched her lower leg over the bluestone gutter and, once on her feet, pulled her cardigan around her belly. She wasn't just fat after all.

Coral smoothed her hand over the bump. She had loved looking after John, Mrs Dixon's baby, and soon she'd have one of her own, soft, and spotless and new. She was still getting used to the idea, but every moment she felt more confident. Matron Flagg continued to rail at her when she left Spring House, and it surprised Coral how little it affected her. She didn't have to worry anymore about her place there; not being staff, student, resident, or worker. She had her own place in the world now. Mother.

There were only a few steps to navigate to the front door and into the quiet little foyer that served as a waiting area. A nurse soon appeared in the adjoining office doorway. Her starched apron covered most of her light blue dress uniform, and she wore a small white hat pinned to her dark hair.

"Hello, you must be Coral. I'm Sister Kelly."

Coral extended her hand to greet Sister Kelly but offered the wrong hand and dropped her suitcase.

"It's alright to be nervous. All the girls are when they arrive."

Two girls in varying stages of pregnancy waddled past the opening that led into the hallway and waved a hello at Coral. She returned their smiles, and all of Matron Flagg's judgement faded away. They were just like her.

Another girl passed in the opposite direction. "Oh, Isobel?" Sister Kelly strode toward the hallway and called after her. "Can you show Coral around while I complete her paperwork?"

"Of course, Sister." Isobel took Coral's hand and led her away, her shiny blonde hair tied into plaits that reached her waist. "How long have you got to go?"

"The nurse said two months."

"Here's the sitting room, and that's another office." Isobel tapped her overall clad tummy. "I've only got one left. So, I'll probably go before you."

"Go?"

"To hospital. But stranger things have happened around here. Let me tell you." Isobel giggled; she seemed too sweet to be one of those girls the Matron had called 'loose' and 'hussies'. "Here's the kitchen, and the sister's rooms are up there."

A short staircase of dark wood led to the room above them. The carpet strip that ran down its centre did an abrupt turn at the first landing and then disappeared over their heads.

"And here are our rooms." Isobel bowed and swept her hand down the hallway as if she was preparing the way for someone special.

Coral peeked into each room as she passed. Each was almost the same. Four beds and bedside tables, a cupboard and pretty floral curtains, and a wall heater under the window.

"And you're in with us!" Isobel announced as she entered the last room on the left. She plonked herself on her bed, and watched while Coral unpacked her suitcase onto the bed diagonally opposite hers.

Coral was glad she'd bought some new clothes just the week before. Everything was getting so tight.

"Oh, that's nice," Isobel said when Coral opened a tunic to refold it. "The colours are so pretty. I can't find anything as pretty as that. Besides, they just issue us with overalls and aprons."

"They're not that expensive. Just from Bell & Welch in the city. We could go together and—"

A loud chuckle erupted from underneath the blankets on the bed next to Isobel's. Coral hadn't even noticed anyone was there. "Girls are not allowed outside the home! Rule number five hundred and fifty bloody million."

Isabel shushed the blanketed body. "Rose, please don't swear. You'll get in trouble!"

"Yeah, Rule number six million and fifty-two. Girls found smoking or using bad language will be dismissed instantly."

"Wow!" Coral slumped onto her bed. "There are *that* many rules? And you know them all?"

Isabel cupped her hands around her mouth to direct her whisper. "She's been here... *twice*."

Coral didn't care about that, but frowned and shook her head. "We're not allowed outside? At all?"

"There's a courtyard—"

"Yep. There's a courtyard." The girl in the bed across from Coral's sat up and scratched at her short red hair. With her hair so short, she looked more like a boy than a girl. "It's built inside the walls of the house. That way, we can't be seen." She made a big display of her belly. "Coz... Y'know. We can't let the good people of the real world face their delusions."

"Come on, Rosie, you've woken up all grumpy."

"I'm Rose, not Rosie."

"That's because you're all prickly!"

Rose threw a pillow at Isobel, and Isobel giggled and pretended to throw it back at Rose but kept it as a cushion between her back and the iron bedhead. "So, where are you from, Coral?"

Coral thought for a while, not because she didn't know where she'd been, but she didn't know where home was; where she'd actually belonged, or belonged to, or where her people were.

"The department I suppose."

Rose interjected. "Oh look, another one! Me too." She slid off her bed and left the room with a determined waddle.

"I'm from the country," Isobel explained. "A place called Creswick. It's near Ballarat."

"I've heard of Ballarat before."

She giggled again. "No one knows I'm here."

"No one at all?"

"Well, my family, of course, but they're all sworn to secrecy. Everyone else thinks I'm in the city doing a fancy office course. The sisters here are really kind and when they're not busy, they let me practice my typing in the office."

Coral was confused. "So you *are* doing the course, then?"

"No silly. It's just so when I go back home, I can say I didn't like the course after all, but I learned to type, so it wasn't a complete waste."

"What about your baby?"

Isobel's eyes lost their shine. "It's not really mine. Not really. I mean, I can't take it home with me. I don't want to take it home. Some lovely couple in Melbourne will adopt it. That's what they've told me."

"Thanks, Sister!" Rose waved a piece of paper at someone further down the hallway and shuffled back into the room. "Seeing as you didn't know the rules, I got 'em for you on paper. That way, you don't have to listen to me prattle on about them constantly."

"But that's all you do anyway, Rose."

"Maybe if I complain enough, they'll change 'em."

"Not likely."

Coral scanned the rules and became so overwhelmed she sat on the bed.

Feed babies 6.30 am.
Waiting mothers rise 6.30am.

<u>*Prayers*</u>
Morning 8.40am.
Evening 6.40pm.
No girls must write letters or give them to visitors to post.

Girls may have visitors once per week—Saturday afternoon from 2pm to 4 pm. Visitors must not leave without seeing Matron or Sister.

<u>*Lights*</u>
Nursery lights out at 10.10pm.
All other lights out at 9.30 pm.

Girls must bathe daily.
Baby washing must be finished at 10am.
Girls found smoking or using bad language will be dismissed instantly.
Girls must be obedient and respectful. Overalls and apron to be handed in on discharge.
Girls are not allowed to be outside the home without special permission from the Matron.
Girls must remain for a period of 3 months in the Home after the baby is born.
Beds to be aired on rising and made by 8.30am.

<u>*Maternity home—rules for nursery.*</u>
Time allowed for feeding babies   20-30 minutes and no longer.
Babies must not be fed during the night.
Constipation and sore buttocks must be reported to the matron after 24 hours.
Babies must not be taken out of their cots between feeds.
Babies to be put on stool[1] after each feed.

---

1. Potty training methodology at the onset of the 20th century was simple: Babies would be put on strict laxative schedules to induce pooping at predictable times. Most doctors encouraged caretakers to start this 'training' as young as six months, and it was a philosophy that extended into the late 1940s. Babies would be put on a stool (potty), until they pooped, and their subsequent release from the stool was their 'training'.

Coral put the sheet of paper on her dwindling lap. "But what if—"

"Rules are rules Coral. Just follow 'em and get out of here as soon as you can."

"Don't listen to Rose. The sisters are quite nice, really. And you'll get used to the rules, I promise."

Saturday 20th March, 1948— City Mission Maternity Home, Albion Street, East Brunswick

Coral's first night was one of broken sleep and strange dreams. Babies cried in her dreams, riding on the seeds of dandelions off into the night. She tried to chase after them, but the wind was too strong. The wind didn't quiet their pitiful, desperate cries, and she could still hear them when she woke... from the nursery on the other side of the courtyard.

All the girls met for breakfast in the large dining room. Instead of one menu, different meals were on offer. Dry toast for those not feeling well, weetbix, normal toast with jam, and fried eggs. Coral collected her toast and jam and watched the girls begin their day. Some were quiet, some chatty; all different sizes and hairstyles, but somehow made the same by their swollen bellies and the need to be behind the big door, never to be seen.

"Janey's due home today, isn't she?" A voice further down the table asked.

Isobel nudged Coral. "That's right, she is. She had her baby a couple of days ago. You'll really like her. Janey's a nice girl."

"Will her baby come home too?"

Isobel used her spoon to draw a slow circle in her weetbix. "I don't think so."

Coral spent her morning with the Mothercraft Nurses. She watched them teach the new mothers how to bathe their babies and listened to their talk about medicine and colic. Not all the girls attended the classes. Not all of them needed to know about washing babies' clothes and the best way to get them off to sleep. Others simply hadn't made up their minds yet. Coral paid close attention and asked lots of questions. No one was taking her baby from her.

The dorms were dark, and the streetlights crept in to outline the furniture and not much else at all. All the bodies in all the beds couldn't sleep, they lay awake with their thoughts, and kept silent vigil to Janey's tears. Sobs come from other rooms too. Perhaps her cry ignited the grief in another. But this was the only place in the world she could share her grief. No one else would understand.

Coral turned over and moved her belly into a more comfortable position. Babies don't always make people happy, another thing that wasn't true after all. This place was sad. Babies cried for mothers and mothers cried for babies. And there was no way for her to escape any of the longing.

Rose sneaked alongside Coral's bed and sat near her back. She rubbed Coral's shoulders and back, like someone nice at the Depot once did. She couldn't remember that lady's name anymore. It was a lifetime ago.

Rose wiggled closer to Coral and lay on the bed. It was a struggle to fit bellies and bodies on the one mattress, but they managed. Rose whispered, "They cry because they gave part of their heart away. It always hurts. Labour hurts their bodies, and then their hearts are ripped open. If they can survive all that pain, maybe their minds will stay intact."

"Are you keeping your baby, Rose?"

"Not on your Nelly![2] I'm one of those girls they describe on their forms as being 'satisfied' I'm making the right choice for the child. But some girls never get over it. Others feel they didn't get a choice at all."

"I thought we had a choice."

"Not always."

"I don't get it."

"Take Isobel. She can't go back to her family with a baby in tow. Small town. They'd ruin her life. Her boyfriend ran off to Indonesia or somewhere as soon as he heard. He wasn't even with her to face her family, the turd. Her family sent her here. They haven't told the boyfriend's family, less gossip that way."

"So she goes home and pretends none of this happened?"

"Look at her. She's so broken that she can pretend anything. Didn't you notice? All that giggling. Her life has made her mental already. Betrayal will do that sort of thing. I'm sure he said he loved her and all that other stuff they say. Then what happens? The family locks her up 'for her own good' until she learns to be a good girl."

"And he went to Indonesia. Fighting?"

"Peacekeeping or some crap. He's never even sent her a letter. I don't even believe he's in Indonesia, myself. Just off living the life of Reilly[3] while she gets drowned in shame."

"Does her family come to visit?"

"What do you think? She'll be paying for this for the rest of her life."

Coral folded her pillow to make it more comfortable. Somehow Isobel's giggles had lost part of their sweetness.

Friday 16th April, 1948—
City Mission Maternity Home, Albion Street, East Brunswick

---

2. Never!

3. An easy life.

"What's going on?"

A bunch of the girls were leaning over each other to see out the side window.

"Lady Bradbury's here." Rose draped her body over the arms of the lounge chair and performed a regal wave.

Bradbury. Coral's heart leapt. "Like Matron Bradbury?"

"Keep ya pants on[4], love. It's the premier's wife, doing her thing. Civic duty or something."

Coral squished her way through the gaggle of girls and made sure the lace panel remained undisturbed over the window. Reporters jostled outside the low fence with their writing pads and flash cameras that were so big it took two hands to hold them. They were focused on the lady who posed with a shovel for the first turning of the sod. She wore a beautiful outfit and from the back, it looked like she was at ease with all those cameras and the reporters smiled and asked her questions.

"Sixteen thousand pound. That's what they're spending." Rose called.

"On what?"

"A new toddler's home."

Coral thought it was a great idea, although she could think of so many places that could use 16 thousand pounds. She couldn't even imagine what that amount looked like. Rose reached for something in the bookcase with her foot, but only managed to flick the book to the floor. She groaned when she had to move to pick it up and then lay back into the chair, legs over one arm, shoulders against the other.

"Don't worry Coral. You're not gonna miss anything. They keep it all in this scrapbook."

"What's in it then?"

"Stuff to make them feel good."

Isobel slapped the top of Rose's head as she passed and sat next to them. "It's not. Stop being silly. It's about all the ways this house helps the girls."

---

4. Be patient.

"Hey, they've added something new." Rose opened the scrapbook wide and sat properly in the chair. "It's from the Herald in March."

"Are there any photos?"

"Of us? You're pulling my leg, right?"

All the girls reacted in some way to Rose's comment. All that hiding, behind the big door and the curtains, pretending you don't exist, took a toll on all of them. Some looked down faced at Rose's comment, others laughed it off. Babies started crying in the nursery. Some mothers checked the time and disappeared, others stayed and cried for the babies they couldn't feed. Among the babies crying and the girls crying, Rose read the article.

"... With its pleasant garden, airy sitting rooms and attractive bedrooms, there is an atmosphere of rest and cheerfulness. Inmates arrive three months before their babies are born (they go to the Women's Hospital for their confinements) and return for three months afterwards with their babies. Many are adopted, and there is always a waiting list of people wanting to take them. In special cases, babies may be kept until 18 months old. If a mother wishes to take her baby, all efforts are made to help her to find a position, so that she may support it..."

"See this, Coral?" Rose asked as her regal hand swept the living room. Girls sobbed into hankies, babies cried in the distance, arms folded against sullen faces, and Isobel giggled at the chaos. "See... it's an atmosphere of rest and cheerfulness."

Tuesday 20th April, 1948—
City Mission Maternity Home, Albion Street, East Brunswick

Coral called from the foyer down the hallway. "She's here!"

Isobel stepped out of the car and made her way gingerly to the front door of the maternity home. Her enormous belly was gone, and a loose dress draped over her form. Coral greeted her at the door and Rose took her hospital case from her hand. "How was it?"

"It was okay. Hurt like the blazes[5], but the baby will be alright and have a good home. I expect that's all that matters."

Her eyes didn't sparkle, and Coral expected her to giggle at any moment. "Did you find out what it was?"

"I didn't ask, and they didn't tell me. I think it's better this way, anyway. It'll stop me from daydreaming, and thinking of names and wondering…"

Rose leant her head close to Coral's. "No, it won't. Poor love."

Sister Kelly appeared from the office. "Yes, it's best to think of the wonderful life you've given your child. You still need to rest, my dear. Sitting room, or bedroom?"

"I think the sitting room for now."

"Good-o. Coral, can you help her into the sitting room?"

Rose took Isobel's suitcase to their room and Coral offered her arm for Isobel to hold while she toddled to the sitting room.

"Oh Coral." Isobel said, "I left my magazine in the suitcase. Could you get it, please?"

"Of course. Back in a tick." Coral entered their dorm to find Rose transferring all her handkerchiefs to Isobel's bedside table. "Want mine too?"

Rose nodded. "Tonight's gonna be a tough one."

---

5. Hell

Saturday 15th May, 1948—
City Mission Maternity Home, Albion Street, East Brunswick

Coral couldn't get comfortable. That wind pain was getting worse. What was it? The potatoes? She'd eaten potatoes before. Why would it annoy her now? But that's what she'd thought about those oranges last week; and they were a *pain*.

She tried sleeping in different positions, visiting the bathroom, and sipping water. The ache only went away long enough for Coral to drop off to sleep, and then it woke her again. Was she sleeping for an hour between each bout, or hours at a time? She slipped out of bed and stood in the kitchen, bare feet on the linoleum and watched the clock. Coral buckled over when the next pain hit. It must be because she was standing. It was never that bad in bed. When her pain was over, she searched cupboards for the Enos[6], but another pain made her clench the kitchen table and give up on her search. She was in labour.

She'd only just made it back into her room as the next one came. "Oww," she groaned and clutched her belly.

Rose jumped from her bed and grabbed at her belly, too. "Oww."

"Oww," Coral continued, "That was a longer one."

"Oww" Rose complained.

"Stop it, you idiot! This really hurts!"

Sister Kelly appeared in her dressing gown. "What's going on in here?"

Coral hung onto the wall. "I think it's my time, Sister."

"Ow, mine too!" Rose now clutched the end of her bed.

The sister waved Rose away. "Stop being silly, Rose. Get back to bed while I attend to Coral."

"But…"

"Coral dear, take a deep breath. We'll call a car for you."

---

6. Sparkling antacid powder

"Ugh!" Rose grunted and a splash of fluid ran down her legs and across the floor. "Told ya!"

Sister's mouth opened and closed like a fish. "Look at the mess you've made. Honestly, Rose, what will we do with you?"

"I dunno," Rose panted. "Send me to the hospital, maybe?"

Coral laughed, and Rose joined in, but they soon moaned and cradled their bellies again.

Saturday 15th May, 1948—
Royal Women's Hospital, Carlton

Coral's eyes flickered over all the white sleeping bundles lined up in the nursery, but she only had eyes for one basket. Her tight round belly was gone, replaced by a smaller pudge of stretched skin and relaxed muscles. She still rubbed her tummy sometimes, but her heart now lived outside her body, on the other side of the big glass window.

Roses's face appeared at her shoulder. "Okay, so where is he?"

Coral pointed through the glass, a smile on her face. "That one. Back row, second from the right."

"What did you call him?"

"Rodney Graeme."

"Nice." Rose turned and leant on the glass. "They won't let you keep him, you know."

"What a horrible thing to say, Rose!"

"I'm just the one being realistic here."

"They said I could keep him. Why would they change their minds?"

"What's your number?"

Coral's shoulders slumped.

"You're a home girl, right? We can spot each other a mile off, and so can others. So, what's your number? Tell me what it is and I'll tell you something straight after."

Coral sighed and looked down at her slippered feet. "66420." She mumbled, and tears pricked her eyes.

"There you go, your number is 66420, and right now you have a sick feeling in your stomach and it's not because you've just had a baby."

"But I'll never walk out on him. They won't take him from me."

"That's a nice thought ya got there, love. But they always win."

"Who's *they*?"

"All of them. The ones with all their forms and rules." Rose looked across all the baskets to little Rodney. "What kind of life can you give him, anyway? Best to have him adopted by some better couple. Better than us anyway."

A tear slid down Coral's cheek. "Better than us?" she sighed. "That's everyone on earth, isn't it?"

"That's what they *want* us to believe. But if you think about it, none of what they tell us makes sense. They treat us like we're stupid. Only it's not that we're stupid, we just don't know stuff. They don't teach us the things that families do; like opening bank accounts. We have to suffer the humiliation of always being treated like we're a sandwich short of a picnic[7]. But somehow that's our fault too. When everything goes to shit, we're the ones in the wrong because of our... what did they call it again? Moral Decay."

"Moral Decay?"

"It's what they labelled *me* as. You get knocked up by your employer's husband, brother, or son, and we're the ones that are shamed, blamed, and shoved aside. Then they make us give pieces of our hearts away until there's nothing left to give away anymore. That's what we are, Coral, delinquents. Morally bankrupt. And we weren't the ones who did anything wrong."

"The matron at Spring House said I was 'of dubious morality'. I don't even know what that means."

"It all means the same thing, don't it? They have to find a way to make it our fault. That way, they get to punish *us* for *their* sins."

"The sisters never told me not to do it."

---

7. Stupid

7. Stupid

"That's coz they just don't get it." Rose smiled, then snorted. "They never get it—get it?"

Coral smiled, but there was sadness wedged deep inside her heart.

Rose nudged her. "Nah, we're like those polishing rags they made us wax the floor with at the Depot. Did you hafta do that?"

Coral nodded and felt sure her knees ached just hearing the words.

"We work hard to make them look good, but we're the ones that are left with the tarnish stains that never come out. And it's our fault for being made dirty, somehow."

"Life is strange."

"Life is a piece of shit." Rose gazed on all the white cocooned bundles in their baskets. "I had another little girl. And I know for a fact–complete truth, Coral–she will be safer with a family than becoming a ward like me. I just hope life is kinder to her."

"Would you have kept her if you had the chance?"

"Probably not. Look at me, what could I offer her?"

"What about her father?"

"They keep telling me to shut up about that. Well, it's either the husband or the son of my employer. Same as last time. They tell you you're disgusting, but they take you back to *rehabilitate* you. Can't bring shame to your employers now, can you? Seems I'm there to wait on the house, and then after dark, wait on her men. They can all go to hell!"

"Shh, Rose."

Two women admiring babies further down the window gasped at Rose's outburst and turned away from the girls, but not before looking them up and down. Rose stood taller and Coral took her by the arm before she could say or do anything. "C'mon Rose, let's go back to our room; time for a cup of tea."

"Oh my God, will the whole world stop tutting at us for once? Did they all take tutting lessons?"

Coral waddled back to the window and blew Rodney a kiss, then re-joined the still muttering Rose.

"How come *we* didn't get to take tutting lessons?"

Tuesday 13th July, 1948—
C.W.D. Flinders Street Railway Building

"Mr Oxford, look! It's the letter we've been waiting on." Mrs Shaw hastily opened the envelope. "It's all well and good for Sister Kelly to tell us about a phone conversation, but once we have it in letter form, it's official. Now we can get to work."

The Secretary
Children's Welfare Department
Flinders St
Melbourne

Dear Mrs Shaw,
Re—Coral Gladys Maxwell. A domestic position has been secured for her with Mrs Hazel Murray, on a property outside Nhill, Victoria.
Mrs. Murray is willing to take both Gladys and her child. And train Gladys in general home duties.
She is due to leave the home on August 18th, 1948, and I would be glad if you would advise me whether it is in order for her to go on that date, and whether or not she would be accompanied by anyone from the department.
Thanking you,
Yours faithfully,
Sister Kelly (Matron)

Monday 19th July, 1948—
C.W.D. Flinders Street Railway Building

Ding!

Mrs Shaw pushed the typewriter carriage back to the left and prepared to sign off. She wondered if this might be the most satisfying letter she'd ever written. She wanted to cross her fingers, rub a rabbit's foot, or do something equally superstitious. All that stood between the past and a new life for Coral was the enclosed application form.

Mrs H. Murray
'Fairview'
Via Nhill

Dear Madam,
Re- Coral Maxwell
I have been informed by the Matron of Melbourne City Mission Maternity Home that you are prepared to employ the above-named state ward who is due to leave the home mentioned on the 15th proximo. I shall be glad of your confirmation in this regard and if you will compete and return to this department the enclosed application form.

Sunday 1st August, 1948—
City Mission Maternity Home, Albion Street, East Brunswick

Life at the Maternity Home was one blurry day after the other. Coral took every mothercraft class she could and learned so many more things than what Mrs Dixon had taught her while she cared for baby John. She learnt all about bathing, feeding, nappies, washing and medicines. Each class meant she got to hold Rodney that little bit longer, but all the sisters were very stern about their rules on how you should raise a child.

They kept referring to a book called the *Mothercraft Manual*. Rose said it was some *fuddy-duddy text* more than 25 years old, but to Coral it was the only book she'd heard of that told her how to keep Rodney safe, and the sisters were always so confident in their methods.

Strict regularity, they kept telling her, would do Rodney the world of good. Without it, he might become hysterical, or an imbecile, develop epilepsy, or any other form of degeneracy or conduct disorder in adulthood! Coral didn't even know what some things were, but they sounded terrifying. The sisters reminded her that regular habits would secure a lifetime of good health and a firm moral character for Rodney. She nodded along with them, but still got in trouble almost every day.

"Coral! Stop cuddling that baby this instant!"

Coral did as she was told, but wondered why it always stung her heart so much to be a 'good' girl.

Coral ran from the kitchen and fixed a band aid to her hand. She wouldn't miss this for the world, and a careless slip up with a knife and an apple wasn't going to keep her away.

Isobel stood nervously in the foyer, hat in place, and her gloved hands holding her suitcase. "Well, I suppose this is it."

"It is." Rose offered her a warm hug. Coral watched, knowing that one hug was filled with every emotion she could list, or experience. They had been through the worst of times together and may never hear from each other again. Deep friendships placed in another little compartment tucked away from the world, never to be spoken aloud. The sisters watched on; they'd gathered to offer their farewells too.

"Coral," Isobel wiped tears from her eyes, "You promised us you'd read that letter you got yesterday, remember? I'm not leaving until you do."

Coral thought about not reading it at all, and keeping Isobel there forever, but retrieved the letter from her overall pocket. "I've been carrying it everywhere", she smiled. She cleared her throat and read...

Dear Gladys,

We were all so pleased to receive your letter and photos. What a nice one of you and Rodney. The children could not look at them long enough and Alice said I wish Gladys would come tonight and Joseph often asks when you are coming----it won't be so long now will it?

Are you fond of children Gladys? I hope you will be able to settle down and feel at home and take an interest in helping me keep the home nice. If you are happy with us, you might grow to be like an older sister to the children and Rodney like a little brother. Joseph is always wanting me to buy him a little brother. If you are a good girl, you will always have a home with us and you would not mind if we love Rodney, will you? As we all love little babies very much.

Joseph is a strong willed lively little boy, and he takes a bit of handling sometimes, but he has his lovable ways and can be a real little man if he likes and he loves babies. Alice has her determined little ways too, but she is a sweet little soul. You will know my husband when he meets you at Nhill. He is not tall, but very kind and cheery. He is middle-aged and wears glasses and is very fond of babies.

Rodney is evidently doing very well and gaining weight nicely.

We are having our kitchen repaired and the man is very busy so we are not sure when it will be finished and we have just received our refrigerator after waiting a long time, we will be set for the summer.

And now I must retire.
Good night, dear.
God bless you.
Yours sincerely,
H. A. Murray
P.S. Alice is going to give you a big hug.

Rose and Isobel stared wide eyed at Coral.

Rose's mouth dropped open. "Strike a light[8] Coral! You've got it all."

"I have?"

Isobel dropped her suitcase and took Coral in a tight embrace. "Your baby, now a home and a position. And people who genuinely want you. You have it all, and I'm trying my hardest not to hate you!" she said through her tears. "How could it get any better for you?" Isobel took Coral's hands and spoke directly into Coral's eyes. "I'm forever going to imagine you living a very happy life on a farm with your darling little Rodney. What a beautiful story."

Coral kissed her cheek. "You get to go home to your people now and take care of yourself."

Rose wiped her nose. "Yeah, and show 'em how good you are at typing!"

---

8. Wow!

The Sisters chuckled with the girls and used their hankies to wipe their eyes. "Best of luck Isobel," they called.

And the door closed quietly behind her.

Monday 2nd August, 1948—
C.W.D. Flinders Street Railway Building

Mrs Shaw removed her hat as she entered the office. "Was that Detective McLaren I passed in the hallway just now?"

Mr Oxford's chair squeaked as he leant back into it. "It was. He stopped in to produce the files we were after about the carnal knowledge aspect of Coral Maxwell's case."

"Any news since last month's visit?"

"No. He's still not prepared to accept her version of events, and Matron Flagg hasn't been helpful at all. He's hung up on some 'conflicting statements' Coral made about the parentage of her child and the man called 'John'."

Mrs Shaw felt the tension ride across her shoulders. "Of course Coral made conflicting statements. She didn't even know how she got pregnant!"

"And that is how his investigation has ended, I'm afraid."

"It's ended?"

"Detective McLaren's decided that further enquiry is useless, and the issue of a warrant, futile."

Mrs Shaw's handbag landed on her desk with a thump. "I do see his point, Mr Oxford. I really do. But they're looking in the wrong place. There's no point chasing some man she was with when she was already four months pregnant!"

"Oh, and there's a letter from Dobson on your desk."

"Just what I need on a chilly morning, Mr Oxford, a bit of heat from the secretary of the department."

"What do you think it's about?"

"Honestly, I have no idea. We've got too much on our plate already."

Re—Coral Maxwell.

It appears there is a sum of £114 to the credit of this ward. £145 credit to her brother Allan, and £108 to her brother Ronald. Such credits, being the surplus of military payments, were the result of their father's enlistment in the forces.

Apparently, no attempt has been made to use this money to Coral's advantage and as a matter fact, we allowed East Kew Girl's home to outfit her when she went on service in February 1946 at a cost of £15/7/0 (towards which, the state presumably confiscated £5) She should have been outfitted from her savings.

It's not clear from the file whether the girl knows of this credit, whether it is undesirable to let her know now, or whether it is possible at this late stage to expend it to her advantage whilst she is still a ward.

Does the same situation apply with respect to the brothers, Allan and Ronald?

As Coral is due to leave City Mission on 15.08.48 to service with a woman at Nhill, we should contact her immediately about her financial affairs.

Could she come into the office?

Are service conditions to apply with Mrs Murray of Nhill, and is she a registered service applicant?

Wednesday 4th August, 1948—
C.W.D. Flinders Street Railway Building

Mr Oxford placed a cup of hot tea on Mrs Shaw's desk. "I phoned the Matron of the City Mission Maternity Home for Coral to come to the

Department. Coral has an infected hand and is seeing a doctor today, but she'll be here either tomorrow or on Friday."

"That's one task out of the way. I appreciate it." Mrs Shaw sipped at her tea and closed her eyes. "While you're at it, can you chase up our good friend Matron Flagg once more?"

"I suppose it's that time again."

"Perhaps the good Lord will prompt her to pay Coral's unpaid wages *this* time."

John flipped his calendar with his pen. "It *has* been five months now."

"We shouldn't be cynical, Mr Oxford, but perhaps it's time to mention we shall refer the matter to the Crown for collection, if she doesn't pay?"

Mr Oxford drew a sheet of typing paper from his desk drawer with a flourish. "I shall add that particular note with pleasure, Mrs Shaw."

Friday 6th August, 1948— *C.W.D. Flinders Street Railway Building*

"You'll miss your tram, Coral." Sister Kelly watched Coral pace and bite her bottom lip. "Here, take my wristwatch; then you'll know how long you've been away, and how long until his next feed. We'll take care of him for you. The quicker you go, the quicker you'll get back."

Coral stepped out into the cold August morning and headed along Albion Street to the tram stop on Sydney Road. Sister Kelly was right; she only just made it to the tram in time.

The morning sun cast shadows across the face of the Flinders Street Railway Buildings, but they still looked impressive. Coral rode the elevator to the second floor and took a jagged breath as the doors opened on the busy reception desk of the Children's Welfare Department.

"Can you please make sure this makes today's post, Janet?" a man passed an envelope to the lady behind the desk, and then disappeared down a long hallway.

"How may I help you?"

"Coral Maxwell, to see Mr Oxford."

"Yes, please take a seat."

Janet spoke to another young lady passing her desk. "Could you please let Mr Oxford know Miss Maxwell is here to see him?"

Miss Maxwell. Coral couldn't remember being called Miss Maxwell before. She straightened her back and tucked her feet under the chair, crossing her ankles as she did. Something was missing. She checked her hat was still pinned in place. She hadn't forgotten her jacket and her shoes matched. Her purse was right beside her. Something was definitely missing. Was it something she needed for Mr Oxford? Some papers perhaps?

Coral took a deep breath. *It was Rodney.*

He'd been there every morning for the last three months, and it was only today she felt him missing from her arms, but not from her heart.

"Coral Maxwell?" Mr Oxford stood above her with his hand extended.

"Oh, um, yes." She replied, woken from her fixation on Rodney.

"Pleased to meet you," he said as he shook her hand. "This way." Mr Oxford gestured to the long hallway.

His office was simple but nice, with a second vacant desk near the arched window. "Coral, this is Mr Dobson, the Department's secretary."

"How do you do?" Coral shook his hand and took her seat opposite the two men.

"He has some questions for you, too. Merely for paperwork purposes, you understand."

Coral nodded, but she still wasn't sure why she had been summoned to the offices in the first place. She checked the sister's wristwatch.

Mr Oxford folded his hands together on the desk. "We, at the department," he said, acknowledging Mr Dobson with a nod, "understand your definite wish is to retain the care of your baby, a boy, who was born on 15th May 1948."

"Rodney."

"Yes. Rodney." Mr Oxford flipped through some papers. "His health is satisfactory, I see."

Coral nodded.

"Now about this appointment to Nhill."

"I have a letter." Coral rummaged through her purse and produced the letter she read to the girls nearly a week before.

Mr Oxford read it, smiled, and nodded his head. "So, you're keen to take the position?"

"Yes, very keen Mr Oxford."

"What do you think, Mr. Dobson?"

Mr Dobson was an older man with white whiskers he trimmed into a short beard. The chain of his pocket watch looped into his waistcoat, and he rubbed at his bulbous nose with a handkerchief. What a fuddy duddy. Didn't he know everyone was wearing wristwatches now? But he spoke in a serious tone, and Coral focused entirely on that.

"Now Coral," he began. "As the department secretary, I can approve this placement with Mrs Murray, but we're yet to confirm what wage she is prepared to pay. Tentative arrangements are that you'll proceed to Nhill on Saturday, the 14th. Will that suit you and your child?"

"Yes, Mr. Dobson."

"That is, if we believe the wages offered are suitable."

"Yes, Mr. Dobson."

"Now, to move on to our next item on the agenda, we must tidy up your board payments at the City Mission before you can go."

He shuffled some files and Mr Oxford pulled notes from a file and tapped at them. "It says here, Coral's been receiving a sickness benefit, and a maternity allowance. The total being held at the Maternity Home is now 11 pounds."

"Good," Mr Dobson announced. "That'll cover your board there. Now Coral, are both you and Rodney well equipped in regard to your clothing?"

Coral nodded, then quickly added, "Oh, may I have some money to buy overalls and a suitcase?"

The two men looked at each other. "Yes, I'm sure we can arrange that."

Mr Oxford wrote a note and handed it to Coral. *Please give this girl £5 from her savings.* "Show that to Janet on your way out and she'll organise it all for you."

Coral looked at her watch again.

"Speaking of money," Mr Dobson interrupted, "Before you go, I must inform you that your current savings, from your domestic positions, and from previous military payments, now totals 114 pounds."

"One hundred and fourteen pounds!! Strike a light!" Coral was gobsmacked. The two men smiled at each other and then chuckled as Coral composed herself. "What I mean to say is..." she sat up tall and straightened her skirt. "... that is indeed wonderful news."

"The department is waiting to hear back from Mrs Murray about your wage. If the conditions of your employment are satisfactory, we'll let you know, and you can call again on the 13th to receive money for fares, etc."

"Have you heard anything about my brothers, Ronald and Allan?"

"We'll look into making sure you have their correct addresses before you leave."

Coral handed the note to Janet at the reception desk and drifted into her own world. Rose and Isobel were right!

I have Rodney. I've been offered a miracle position so I can keep him. Nothing can stop us! Coral wished Isobel was right in front of her now.

How could it get any better for you?

It just did Isobel.

One hundred and fourteen times better!

Monday 9th August, 1948—
C.W.D. Flinders Street Railway Building

Mr Oxford strode past Mrs Shaw in the hallway. "Sorry, can't stop." he lifted his briefcase. "Due in court at 10. I've left a note on your desk."

Mrs Shaw,
Letter from Mrs Murray to the department discussing Coral's wage being set at £1 per week. Mrs Murray considered good employer by the sister at the maternity home.
Girl to commence Monday 17$^{th.}$ 20 shillings per week, OP 2/6.

Goodbye City Mission

To the Secretary,
Dear Sir,
    I am quite prepared to take this young girl and her baby and provide them with a good home, we are on the land and have plenty of good milk etc, and if the girl values her chance, we are prepared to keep them permanently.
    Trusting this is satisfactory,
Yours faithfully,
Mrs. H. A. Murray

<u>Wire sent 13.08.48</u>
Coral travelling morning train Saturday.
Please meet child.

Nhill

1948

Sunday 15th August, 1948—
'Fairview', Via Nhill

The train let out its last puff of steam like an enormous sigh. Coral felt the same. It was the longest train trip of her life, and she was grateful to get out of her compartment. A short tug released her suitcase from the iron luggage rack above her head and it landed with a soft thud on the upholstered bench seat below. Rodney didn't notice the tremor. He was oblivious, sleeping soundly within his swaddled blanket.

The platform was well lit for a country town; people greeted each other by the slatted seats, others headed through the gates for a quick getaway. Coral moved toward the small portico that covered the ticket office and the exit. She took her time. With sleeping Rodney in one arm and her other hand holding her suitcase, there was no room for any kind of incident.

"That must be him," she whispered to Rodney. A bespectacled man stood with his hat in his hands just outside the bustle of the exit. Mrs Murray was right. He was rather short, but he did look kindly.

"Coral Maxwell?"

"Hello, Mr Murray. We're pleased to meet you."

Tuesday 17th August, 1948— 'Fairview', Via Nhill

The morning was sunny, yet bitterly cold winds howled around the brick homestead. Within its walls, all was warm and welcoming. Not just the fire in the hearth, but the Murrays too. In the past days, Coral and Rodney had received more care and attention than Coral thought possible.

The sun shone through the new lace curtains and dropped its patterned light onto the kitchen table. Mr Murray was always in the fields by breakfast time, which left the seated children, toast in hand, to welcome Coral to Tuesday with wide grins.

Mrs Murray scooped fried eggs from the frying pan. "How did you sleep, Coral? I mean Gladys."

"Mummy," Joseph asked, "Is her name Coral or Gladys?"

"Why don't you ask her yourself, Joseph, but remember your manners."

Joseph thoughtfully chewed his mouthful. "If I may ask..." he confirmed he'd begun correctly accepting the nod from his mother. "Is your name Coral or Gladys?"

"Hmm," Mrs Murray tapped Joseph's shoulder. "Perhaps it might be better to ask someone what they *prefer* to be called."

Joseph had had enough of his impromptu social lesson, and bit into his toast and spoke with the wad rolling around in his mouth. "So what's your name?"

"Joseph!"

Despite Mrs Murray's stern face, Coral laughed; and so did his mother. "Whatever am I going to do with you, Joseph?"

Mrs Murray sat a cup of tea down for Coral. "*Do* you have a preference?"

"I do like the name Gladys very much. But you can call me whatever you prefer."

"Did you hear that, children? This young lady prefers to be called Gladys."

Little Alice waved from her seat at the end of the table. "Good morning, Gladys."

"Good morning, Alice."

The land at Fairview was flat and green, and not a rolling hill in sight. 'Green now,' Mr Murray had said on her first morning, 'but the last couple of years, it was dry and brown.'

"Sheep or crops?" she'd asked him to make polite conversation.

Mr Murray seemed surprised at her question.

"I spent some time in Gippsland; Jeetho."

"Ah, that's some nice land there. Here, I run a bit of both. The land north of us is good for sheep, and as you move south, the soil gets less sandy, and better for crops. We're in the middle, so I run both. Bit of a safeguard too if one does better than the other, and things are just coming good now after the war and that uncertainty. Only good times ahead, Gladys, don't you say?"

Coral nodded. That seemed a very good thing to believe.

With the cold licking at her ankles, Coral tried imagining brown as far as she could see, but the horizon got all wavy until she couldn't see it properly at all. The wind stung at her eyes. That's where the wind came from too; a flat horizon with nothing to stop it. She turned the lever that secured the wire door of the chook shed.

Coral fumbled her hands under the warm hen and rushed the eggs into the kitchen.

"Four eggs! That's perfect." Mrs Murray pulled out the mixing bowls. "Let's get to work making Mr Murray's birthday cake before he's back from the paddocks."

Under Mrs Murray's direction, Coral collected the flour from the larder. "What was that awful noise last night?"

"I didn't hear any awful noises, and don't you worry about disturbing us; even when I hear Rodney at night, it makes me smile."

"It was a kind of scratchy and metal sounding. I woke up and looked over at Alice's bed, but she was fast asleep."

"Probably the old windmill. It's only noisy when the wind is at a certain speed. We probably don't hear it anymore." Coral nodded. The sound did keep going and going and going until she thought she was mad!

"Do you have any plans for after your chores are done?"

"I think I'll write to Mrs Shaw at the department today and tell her how we've settled in."

"That's very thoughtful, Gladys."

Coral chuckled. "Might even tell her about that wretched windmill."

Letter from Coral to Mrs Shaw - undated

'Fairview'
Via Nhill

Dear Mrs Shaw,
I hope you received my photo of Rodney and myself. I hope you are well. Rodney and myself are well.

We had a good trip, but Rodney was uneasy. It was a long journey up here. We were going all day, from ten to nine in the morning until about quarter to eight in the night. We missed Saturday's train by half a minute.

It is lovely up here. The fresh air is lovely too. It is terribly cold up here the last couple of days. It is raining now. The children are lovely. Their names are Joseph and Alice.

I am sorry I didn't see you the two days I went into the Welfare as you were not there. I took Rodney in the once.

I haven't much news so I will close with lots of love from Gladys and Rodney.

Please write soon
lots of xxxxxxxx from us.

Sunday 22nd August, 1948—
'Fairview', Via Nhill

On Sunday mornings, the family gathered in the living room to hear Mr Murray read from the Bible, and to sing a hymn or two. Coral wasn't interested in the readings that much, but she loved to sing, and often just enjoyed the family being together. No one working or having pressing chores to attend to. Soon enough, Rodney cried out from Coral's room.

And every Sunday it made Mr Murray laugh, "You could set your watch by that kid!"

"He certainly has got himself into a routine."

"Always at the end of the last hymn, too."

The children giggled and Mrs Murray set to lunch while Coral nursed Rodney. Once he was fed and changed, she brought him into the living room.

Mr Murray held his arms out. "Let me take him. I hardly get to see the fella."

"Gladys, come and have some lunch," Mrs Murray called from the kitchen. Joseph and Alice flew by her in a rush to play with Rodney.

A flush of warmth filled Coral's heart. What a lovely home, and she was so lucky to be a part of it. She didn't mind her chores, even when she had to carry the slops out to the pigs. She thought they were horrible creatures, but Mr Murray told her because she was looking after them, she would get some of the money when they went to the slaughterhouse. The Murrays made even the yucky stuff seem admirable and worth her while.

In a way, it was the same thing with Rodney. No matter how many times her awful world got turned around or upside down, Rodney was there, every morning, needing her.

Bursts of laughter from the living room made her smile while she ate her sandwich.

Mrs Murray placed a cup of tea next to Coral's plate. "So, how are you settling in? Is there anything we can do to help?"

"You've all been so nice to me, and to Rodney."

"But…"

"I'd really like a wristwatch so I can keep an eye on the time with Rodney's feeds."

"That's quite a sensible suggestion."

The kitchen door opened, and Mr Murray strode in with Rodney resting in his arms. Rodney was doing all he could to reach Mr Murray's glasses.

"Arthur," Mrs Murray began, "Gladys would like a wristwatch, and I think it'd be helpful for both of them. What do you think?"

"Oooh, wristwatches are expensive, Gladys. You'll be saving for quite a while."

Coral lowered her chin and her shoulders suddenly felt very heavy. She really wanted one as soon as possible. "Oh, wait!" Her quick response made the Murrays jump, and she smiled. "Sorry. I just remembered. I have money… at the department."

"You do?" Mr Murray raised Rodney to sitting, and his little hands snatched his glasses and pulled them diagonally across his face. "Enough for a wristwatch?"

"Oh yes, Mr Murray! I have more than £100."

Mr Murray spluttered, "Well, that will certainly get you a wristwatch, Gladys! Why, with that kind of money, you could do whatever you want. I'm glad you chose to stay with us."

Rodney squealed with delight as he pulled Mr Murray's glasses from his face, and Coral laughed. "So am I, Mr Murray."

Monday 23rd August, 1948—
'Fairview', Via Nhill

Coral clipped her overall strap in place. Rodney was asleep, and she needed to tend those awful pigs again. She found the slop bucket on the back porch, but before she could lift it, Mrs Murray came through the back screen door.

She held a piece of paper in her hand. "Gladys, I'm writing to the department about your wristwatch. Would you like to hear what I wrote? It's your money, after all."

"Alright,"

"*Dear Mrs Shaw,*

Gladys tells me you might be able to help in a little matter. So, I am writing on her behalf. She says she would like a wristed watch, especially now she has to time Rodney's feeds. They are very pricey up here and there's not much to choose from. She has settled down beautifully and Rodney is well. His little cheeks are becoming quite pink. Gladys is a very sweet mother and is so nice with the children. Would you be able to organise a watch for her?

Yours Sincerely, Mrs. H. E. Murray.

What do you think?"

"I think it's a lovely letter."

"I'll let you know as soon as we hear from them."

Wednesday 25th August, 1948—
C.W.D. Flinders Street Railway Building

Mr Oxford dropped an official envelope onto Mrs Shaw's desk. Its ripped edges meant she wouldn't have to read it herself.

"This is for Coral Maxwell's file."

"And…"

"The department is continuing her guardianship until her birthday next year."

"But she's about to turn 18. I'd bet she's looking forward to being released. What reasons did they give?"

"She has a child, isn't very bright, and she's recently placed herself into service."

"Suppose they don't want to disrupt her now she's finally settled."

"I think that's fair enough, don't you?"

"It'll be nice for her to find a family to rest with for a while."

Thursday 27th August, 1948— 'Fairview', Via Nhill

Coral carefully signed the wages book in the lamplight. *Gladys Maxwell*.

Mrs Murray handed her wages less her savings amount. "What plans do you have for your wages, Gladys?"

"Probably some new clothes. When will we be going to town again?"

"Not for a little while. I'm sorry we're so far from everything. Not much goes on around here, does it?" Tinkering sounds came from the large shed as Mr Murray worked on something mechanical. Bugs flew around the oil lamp he'd perched on the fence nearby.

"No. not really."

Rodney stirred. He'd just been put down, and Mrs Murray went to comfort him. Coral's mouth fell open when she appeared with him in the living room. This broke all the rules in the Mothercraft Manual!

"But Mrs Murray—"

"Shh, Gladys. Trust me. It's alright really." She reclined gracefully into the armchair and rocked him, speaking tenderly. Her fingers played lightly with his hands. Those tiny little chubby fingers that played so earnestly with his toys. She looked over his little fingernails and held his hand in her fingers. "I lost a baby once."

Coral didn't know what to say.

"She was only one. Sweet little Ruthie. The doctors said there was nothing they could do, you see."

Coral couldn't even imagine losing Rodney. She couldn't bear to be away from him at all, let alone if he went to heaven. A lump had formed tight in her throat, but she managed to nod.

"Mr Murray wondered if you might like to stay with us and become part of our family?" Rodney was sleeping now, at complete rest in her arms. "That way, you could settle down and have a true home."

Coral's heart relaxed. Was she dreaming? Someone truly wanted to take care of her for once? Her *and* Rodney. "I think that'd be lovely, Mrs Murray."

"Please Gladys, call me Mum."

Wednesday 1st September, 1948—
'Fairview', Via Nhill

The 'click' of the lamp sounded louder in the dark, its light reflecting from the polished timber bureau. Mrs Murray collected writing paper from its drawer and positioned herself on the tapestried chair. How to start? She'd written the letter a thousand times in her head. A smile crept across her lips. It still surprised her that her husband came up with the idea. He'd been so excited, he'd rubbed his hands together.

Dear Sir,
I am writing to ask you whether we would be able to adopt Coral Maxwell. She has settled down beautifully and is very happy here with us. She is a very nice little girl and we would like to adopt her. We feel that she deserves a good home and someone who would feel like a mother and father to her. She is very keen about it herself and our own two children have grown fond of Coral too. Her baby is growing nicely and he will always be as welcome as his mother.
In the event of an adoption, would it be necessary for the baby to be adopted too or would he just take his place naturally as a grandchild, as his mother, legally adopted, would be our daughter? We would be very happy if you would let us know soon.
Yours Faithfully,
Mrs H. E. Murray

Tuesday 7th September, 1948—
C.W.D. Flinders Street Railway Building

Mr Oxford leant back on his office chair and propped his feet on his desk. The lights of the city were flickering on, and it had been another exhausting day. The letter in his hand crumpled when he put his arms behind his head and sighed. He wouldn't make it to the pub before closing time tonight, and he didn't feel like rushing anywhere.

He'd just read over the Secretary's response to Mrs Murray out at Nhill and dropped the letter to Janet before she'd left for the night.

How delightfully odd. A ward who got passed around, now wanted for adoption. He didn't enjoy typing the letter, knowing it was not what Mrs Murray hoped to hear.

Dear Madam,
Re: <u>CORAL MAXWELL</u>
With reference to your recent letter, it is gratifying to learn that the abovementioned girl has satisfactorily settled down in your home and it is trusted that her good progress will be maintained. Your efforts on her behalf are greatly appreciated but as she is a member of a family and having regard to her past instability, I am of the opinion that consideration on the matter of your legally adopting her should be deferred for the present.
Yours Faithfully, Secretary

Mr Oxford sighed and righted himself in his chair. One more note to go. He dropped the note on Mrs Shaw's desk. She'd be in earlier than he would tomorrow.

From the accountant. Please make available to Mrs Shaw the sum of 9 pound, 7 shillings, and sixpence from girl's savings to purchase a wristwatch for the ward.

Wednesday 8th September, 1948—
C.W.D. Flinders Street Railway Building

Mrs Shaw pulled her coat up against the wind. It wasn't raining yet, but the clouds looked ominous above the tall buildings on Bourke Street. She'd never been so relieved to enter a shop and leave the tension of the hat holding behind.

"May I help you, madam?"

The salesman at Dunklings wore a dark three-piece suit and carried a rather British inflection in his voice.

"Yes, thank you," Dulcie replied. "I'm after a wristwatch, for a young girl."

"A relative?"

Dulcie stretched a small smile across her lips. "Yes. Something like that."

"A lovely choice. I'm sure she'll be thrilled with your selection."

"Thank you. Now, you will send the watch directly to Nhill?"

"Certainly. It's already been registered. We'll have it engraved today, and set the receipt inside the box as you requested."

"Wonderful. Now I just need to write a note and let her know it's on the way."

Friday 17th September, 1948—
'Fairview', Via Nhill

Nhill's main street was wider than any Coral had seen before. Verandas covered the footpath that ran alongside the shops and the family strolled under them together. Just like a proper family. Sometimes Mrs Murray pushed the pram and Coral held Alice's hand. They stopped here and there, chatting with distant neighbours and collecting supplies.

Coral did her best to stay calm and relaxed as they finally approached the post office.

"Go on then!" Mr Murray said, and Coral rushed toward the front door and disappeared inside.

"Over here," Mrs Murray waved from the shady grass where the family sat and waited.

"So what on earth do you have there?" Mr Murray said as she approached.

"It's a wristwatch!" Joseph called before Coral could manoeuvre it from its packaging.

Once free from its wrapping, the silver watch shone when it caught the sunlight. Coral was a little disappointed the silk band wasn't pink or yellow, like she'd seen in some shop windows, but it had some lovely carvings around the face that looked like leaves, or maybe they were scrolls. The face was white with little black numbers and tiny dots for the minute segments. Mrs Murray helped her put it on. "Ah, a black silk band. That's very practical for the work you're doing."

Her very own watch! The children grabbed at her arm to have a look, and Joseph counted the numbers round the dial. They walked back toward the General Store, with Mrs Murray leading the way with the pram. Mr Murray laughed when Coral nearly walked into a tree.

"If you keep looking at it, you'll wear it out!" he joked.

"She's behaving exactly as you did when you got that new tractor, remember?" Mrs Murray called over her shoulder.

Mr Murray laughed again. "And you and your refrigerator."

The General Store was busier than the one at Jeetho. "Is that all you need, Gladys?" Mrs Murray asked.

Coral shifted the new overalls and socks from one arm to the other. "I think so."

"We'll be coming back into town later in the month, so if you forget anything, we can get it then." Mrs Murray guided the children out of the path of other shoppers.

Coral nodded. "Oh wait. There was a doll I wanted to get for...."

Mrs Murray gave a knowing look. "I'll make my purchases and meet you outside."

With all her parcels bundled up, Coral met her family outside the store, and they strolled to the car.

"Gladys, would you like to make some cakes when we get home?" Mrs Murray winked at Coral.

"I'd love to. Is there a special occasion coming up?"

"It's my birthday, it's my birthday!" Little Alice called. "Mummy, Mummy, can Gladys make the little ones that look like butterflies?"

"Would you Gladys? We've got that extra cream from the cow."

"I'd love to."

Monday 4th October, 1948— *'Fairview', Via Nhill*

To the Secretary,

Dear Sir,
I trust you will pardon me for writing to you again, but as I will probably be in Melbourne in about three weeks' time as my little girl needs attention to her eyes, we are wondering whether it is still advisable to consider adopting Coral Maxwell.

She is just as happy and contented as before. In fact more so, she has settled down to the farm life very well indeed and has learned to milk the cows, etc. We find her a splendid little girl altogether, and the children look upon her as a big sister and she calls us Mum and Dad.

Coral is still breastfeeding her baby and he is a lovely little chap and now weighs 14lbs at four and a half months.

If her brothers continue to keep in touch with her, we will be very pleased for them to visit her sometimes. She has not heard from them for a while now.

We will be very pleased to hear from you again soon and to know your decision, and if an adoption is possible, I will be pleased to forward you all details. I do not want a second trip if possible.

Yours Faithfully,
Mrs H. E. Murray.

Thursday 7th October, 1948—
C.W.D. Flinders Street Railway Building

Dear Madam,
Re: <u>CORAL MAXWELL</u>
With reference to your recent letter, I am very pleased to hear that the abovementioned ward has settled down satisfactorily in your employ and apparently she is appreciative of the opportunity you have afforded her.

As previously intimated it is advisable to defer the consideration of legal adoption in Coral's case and when you visit the City this matter will be discussed further with you.

Yours Faithfully,
Secretary

INSPECTOR'S REPORT
Thursday 11th November, 1948—
C.W.D. Railway Buildings, Flinders Street

Suitable home

Coral rooms with her infant, has a very comfortable and well-furnished bedroom shared with employer's daughter, 3yrs.

Coral is happy, wages paid, and healthy.

Scripture study at house with Mrs Murray and family.

Coral seems to be quite happy in this house and to be on very good terms with employer and family who wish to adopt her legally.

Infant well cared for.

Coral is still nursing her babe and seems she is in good condition.

Monday 29th November, 1948—
C.W.D. Flinders Street Railway Building

Mr Oxford walked into the reception area of the Children's Welfare Department and approached the handsome lady in her early 40s who waited there.

"Mrs Murray?"

"Yes."

"I'm Mr John Oxford, one of the officers assigned to Coral Maxwell's case. I understand you wish to speak to the department about adoption?"

Mrs Murray took his hand. "Pleased to meet you."

Mr Oxford guided her down the long hallway towards the office he shared with Dulcie.

Mrs Murray looked into every office they passed. "Gladys.. erm, Coral often speaks of a Mrs Shaw. Is she in the office today?"

"I'm afraid Mrs Shaw was required to attend court today; but I can certainly help with your enquiries."

Mrs Murray set her handbag down beside her chair and Mr Oxford took a seat where he felt most comfortable, behind his desk. "So, Mrs Murray. How are things in Nhill?"

"Most pleasant Mr Oxford. Coral has settled beautifully into farm life on our property, *'Fairview'*. I find she's still a child in many ways and requires firmness but responds very well to kindness and motherly care, as though she has missed it."

"We can only imagine, can't we?"

"Indeed. She's presently having dental treatment with Mr Cole in Nhill, and it will be necessary for her to see my doctor, I think. I'm sure she requires a check-up following the baby's birth. I must organise that when I return."

"Of course. Now you had some questions?"

"Do you know where she stands with her family and if her father will want her back when she is off welfare? It's just that Coral has said she'd like to stay with us instead."

"When her term of departmental control ends, her legal guardianship returns to her father. I would state however, as long as she is living a respectable life and earning her living honestly, he cannot legally compel her to return to his home."

"I see. So she can choose to stay with us, even if she's not legally adopted."

"That's true."

"But we can't legally adopt her, or her child?"

"Although the department doesn't know the whereabouts of Coral's parents, they may appear at a later date and cause all manner of difficulties. You can understand why we would advise your family against adoption."

"Although I'm saddened, I do understand the department's position. She did write to her brothers though, soon after she arrived at *'Fairview'*. They answered once, and the eldest hasn't let her know whether he received the birthday gift she sent him. It worries her."

Mr Oxford opened Coral's file and flipped several pages over. "It's advisable that families keep in touch. Wards are encouraged to write to their relatives. Hmm. It seems in Coral's case; it's not known whether the brothers are aware of the existence of the child."

"Rodney."

"That's right. Rodney. There's nothing noted here."

"Coral said she had written to tell them. Quietly, I had wondered whether they may have turned against her because of the baby. If we can, we'd like to protect her from that and be sure she is happy in our home."

"In my experience, teenage boys are more interested in cricket and football than writing letters, so perhaps it is an oversight on their part, not knowing Coral was waiting for their replies."

"That's true, Mr Oxford." Mrs Murray collected her handbag from the floor, rested it on her lap and sighed. "So, there is no chance of a legal adoption?"

"I'm afraid not Mrs Murray."

Saturday 25th December, 1948—
'Fairview', Via Nhill

Joseph was proud of the Christmas Tree. He'd taken it upon his six-year-old self to find the perfect tree and convince his father to cut it down so he could pot it ready for decorating.

There it sat on Christmas morning, a eucalypt triumph, covered in joyful paper chains. The leaves had dried a little, and some dropped onto the presents below, but they still held the scent of the summer bush.

Mr Murray read the Christmas Story from the Bible, and then everyone opened their presents.

Coral loved the slippers her new Mum and Dad bought her, and Mrs Murray thought the hand cream Coral had gifted her smelled divine. Rodney loved the patterned paper the gifts were wrapped in and scrunched them and squealed with delight.

It was one of the most wonderful Christmas times she had ever experienced.

Goodbye Nhill

'Fairview' Via Nhill
28.01.49

To the Secretary
Children's Welfare Department

Dear Sir,
I am writing to inform you that I cannot keep Coral Maxwell and her baby as we hoped to do, as time goes on Coral is finding the care of her child along with her work rather much and I have her a lot, but I am not well and under my doctor and I find the responsibility of helping Coral care for the baby too much for me and I must think of my husband and children.

Coral is a good girl to work and is clean and trustworthy. She has a loveable nature and is good with the children, but her subnormal condition is such that it requires someone to guide her kindly but firmly along life's highway, especially with the baby, so I am sure you will understand. Coral is afraid that you will take the baby from her and I wonder is it not possible to place her in a babies home or such place where she can work and see her baby too and perhaps have the supervision of a matron or next to that, of course, would be some kindly people such as ourselves who would have better health and more time than I have to help her.

Coral has been with us about five and a half months and the baby is near 8 and a half months old, is cutting teeth, sitting up, and the picture of health and appears in every way a bright normal baby and would win anybody's heart.

My own personal feeling in the matter is that it was a pity the baby was not adopted in the first place. However, Coral is very keen to keep him and I have told her I would ask you to allow her to do so but more than that I cannot do and we must leave it to you.

I will be waiting to hear from you as soon as possible.
Yours faithfully,
Mrs. H. E. Murray.
P.S. We are very sorry to do this but am sure you will understand.

Dear Sir,
Kindly pardon this afterthought, but it might be helpful to you to know that Coral can milk a cow. It is a daily duty here and she likes the outdoor life. She can also make butter. We are on a farm here, and we think a place near some country town where there is a little more life might be better. It is very quiet here, but we don't think it would be good for her to have too much gaiety. She has been a good girl to keep and we would like her to keep in touch with us.
Yours Faithfully,
Mrs. H. E. Murray.

City Mission

1949

Wednesday 9th February, 1949—
C.W.D. Flinders Street Railway Building

Janet appeared at the office door. "Telegram for you, Mr Oxford."
"Thank you, Janet."
Mrs Shaw lifted her head. Telegrams were always cause for concern.
"It's from Mrs Murray in Nhill. She wants to know if we've received her letter about Coral Maxwell yet."
Mrs Shaw nodded. "On Friday." She leant back in her chair and worried the fountain pen in her fingers. "I still don't know what we're going to do about it. I know the department has come to me for suggestions, but..."
"Alright. How about this? I'll return a telegram today. *Your letter received. Reply following.* That should buy us some time."
"That will do, John. Thank you."

Monday 14th February, 1949—
C.W.D. Flinders Street Railway Building

Mr Oxford balanced two cups of tea down the hallway. He'd only spilt a little into one saucer and already claimed that one as his. Pity about the soggy biscuit, though. Hopefully, he could keep Mrs Shaw's dry.

"Tah dah," he announced as he entered the office. "I'm getting better at this." He even managed to not spill the tea when he placed it on Dulcie's desk. "Why the long face, Mrs Shaw?"

"I just got a note from the Secretary."

"And?"

"Coral Maxwell."

"Oh. So, what are we up against?"

"He's saying that all reports indicate that none of the applicants for a service girl are prepared to take a mother and child."

"We knew it was going to be a tough call."

"Are you ready?"

Mr Oxford considered what news Mrs Shaw might have for him and answered her with a long slow blink.

Mrs Shaw put on an officious voice, one that held both resignation and malice. "Knowing Coral and how handicapped she is, my suggestion would be to relieve her of the care of her child under the Infant Life Protection Act. Girl could be well placed then."

"Good Lord."

Neither felt like sipping tea and sat in thoughtful silence. It was Mr Oxford who broke the stillness.

"I don't even know what we can do yet, but can they give us until the end of the week?"

Thursday 17th February, 1949—
C.W.D. Flinders Street Railway Building

"Are you writing to Mrs Murray, or should I do it?"

"You do it John; you've been speaking with her most recently."

Mr Oxford nodded and rolled the paper into his typewriter, joined the two sheets at the top to make sure it was straight, then rolled it back down and typed.

Dear Mrs Murray,

When is it convenient to send the girl and her child to Melbourne, in order that they may be met on arrival? Confidentially, difficulty is being experienced in locating an employer that would be prepared to accommodate both Coral and her infant and it appears probable the child will have to be placed with an approved person and the girl in a suitable situation.

When Coral leaves your employment, will you be so good to forward her wages book, together with any balance outstanding to this department?

Monday 21st February, 1949— 'Fairview', Via Nhill

'Fairview' Via Nhill
21.02.1949

Mr. J. Oxford
Children's Welfare Department

Dear Sir,
Please find wages enclosed. I'm sorry she won't keep her baby. She was very happy here and is leaving with the thought she will be able to keep her baby. I've told her you haven't arranged anything definite. She is in many ways just a child and I'm sure she doesn't realise her position. She seems thrilled at the thought of the journey. I can understand someone not wanting to take on the baby as well, it is a big thing to do. I hope both Coral and Rodney will have good homes.
Yours Faithfully,
Mrs. H. E. Murray

Monday 21st February, 1949—
'Fairview', Via Nhill

"Just drop me off here, Arthur. I can walk to the train station and meet you all there."

"Fair enough." Mr Murray slowed the car to a stop outside the post office and Mrs Murray waved as the car laden with waving hands headed towards the station.

"What can I do for you today, Mrs Murray?"

"I'd like to send a telegram, please."

"Certainly."

Coral travelling Melbourne Train today.
Mrs. H E Murray.

Alice nearly jumped out of her skin when the train's whistle blew as it came into the station. Joseph was fascinated with the smoke and steam and waved his arms around in the air, trying to capture it. Coral would miss the children and their antics so much.

"You've got your sandwiches?"

"Yes, Mum."

Mrs Murray's eyes misted as she wiped imaginary rain from Coral's shoulders. It was cloudy, but no rain was about.

Mr Murray jiggled Rodney in his arms. "And your money for a cup of tea?"

"Yes, Da…. Mr Murray," she said to her feet.

"All aboard!" the stationmaster cried, and the family said their final goodbyes with kisses and hugs and promises to write and stay in touch. It was a quick goodbye, rushed and awkward. Coral was relieved when the train's whistle blew again, and she gave her last waves out the window to the Murray family of four.

"I'm such a different person now," Coral said to Rodney. She'd propped him up in the corner of the bench seat and he smiled and gurgled his answer to her. The train kept with its rhythmic passage through open fields of crops and, at other times, tall trees and wide valleys, and left Coral alone with her thoughts.

When Rodney woke from his naps, she always had more to tell him.

"I've learnt so many new things, haven't I, Rodney? And I was thinking, if we can make it out there in the middle of nowhere, we can do it anywhere, my love. Rose was right. You would have loved Rose. She said I could do anything because I have everything I need. I have you; I have money... but hmm."

Coral's frown made Rodney giggle. She pulled another one just for fun and scooped him into her arms. "We just need a position. I'm sure we'll find another one. This time near the shops, so I can take you for walks in your buggy and people will stop us in the street and admire your chubby cheeks. Yes, they will!"

Coral pulled a spinning top from her pocket. Joseph gave it to Rodney as they left, and Rodney grabbed for it and brought it straight to his mouth. She sat him on the seat and tried to spin it for him, but it wouldn't work.

"And you know what else?" She bent down to kiss his nose. "You'll get to meet Mrs Shaw this time." She tickled him, and Rodney squealed and clapped. "Yes, Hooray!" she clapped along with him.

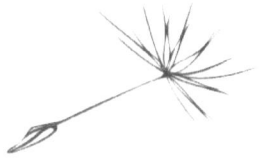

Tuesday 22nd February, 1949—
C.W.D. Flinders Street Railway Building

Mrs Shaw stepped off the elevator and straight in Mrs Dawson's stride. This wasn't the welcome she expected straight from court; the larger woman waving a manilla file in her direction and demanding answers.

"This, uh, Coral Maxwell. I remember that one from the Depot years ago. I'm not surprised she's still in the system. Who collected the child and her infant last night?"

Mrs Shaw pushed her way past Mrs Dawson and into the reception area. "My understanding was that someone from Traveller's Aid met the train and set them up for the night on Flinders Street. They'll be sending them to City Mission in Brunswick this morning."

"Right. As I expected. Well, I've made my report and put it on your desk. Mr Dobson will attend the meeting on Thursday, as will Miss Staines from her babies home."

"Meeting?"

"You'll find it outlined in my report. I've included today's goings on in it as well…. Sister Kelly taking her into the City Mission today, the 22nd, including until such time as a position is found for her. I'll then retain the infant under the Infant Life Protection Part 2. Girl will call at department early on Thursday 24th instance when she may be informed of the situation which will be selected for her. There seems to be no reason why Coral should not be able to earn sufficient to keep herself and pay for her child."

"And after that?"

"Well, that's up to the girl, isn't it?"

Mrs Shaw frowned, caught somewhere between *retain the child* and *informed of the situation which will be selected for her*, and what magic they expected Coral to perform to prove herself worthy.

"Oh, and Dulcie," Mrs Dawson said as she stepped into the elevator, "We won't need you at the meeting."

Mrs Shaw couldn't remember how she got to her office.. She heard the ding of Mrs Dawson leaving via the elevator and sat at her desk and stared at the envelope holding her report.

She couldn't be there for Coral. Her chest constricted and a wave of nausea passed over her, followed closely by relief that she wouldn't have to witness her receiving the news. It washed the nausea away for a moment, then gathered momentum to return as shame for the guilt she felt at being relieved. Dulcie rubbed at her temples but the ache across her forehead wasn't going anywhere.

Thursday 24th February, 1949— C.W.D. Flinders Street Railway Building

Coral stopped and fanned herself one last time against the heat of the summer morning. It was safer to steer the pram she'd borrowed from the Mission with two hands, while Rodney cooed at the people they passed along Flinders Street. Her tram stopped only a block away, but this block seemed to last forever. The foyer of the Railways Buildings felt like cool silk around her, no more baking sun, and squinting eyes.

"Ahh," she sighed to Rodney, "That's better. Here at last."

The elevator doors opened and Coral wheeled Rodney into the reception area. There's that nice lady behind the desk. Janet. Yes, that's what Mr Oxford said her name was.

Janet smiled at her. "You can go down now, Miss Maxwell. They're waiting for you in Mr Oxford's office."

There it was again. *Miss Maxwell.* Coral stood tall and walked Rodney's pram down the long corridor and into the room with the arched windows that looked out over Flinders Street.

But Mr Oxford wasn't there; a man with a bulbous nose sat at his desk, and an older woman with a bun in her hair stood beside him. On the other side of the room, a skinny woman with jet black hair squinted at her from behind her round glasses. A fluorescent light flickered above her and made her glasses twinkle like an off and on switch. Coral smiled and the woman's lips all pinched up as if she'd just tasted a lemon. A change came over her the moment she saw the pram.

"Oh, is this little Rodney? May I?" She didn't wait for Coral's response, threw herself toward the pram and lifted him out. Rodney didn't protest and the chatter from the man distracted Coral, what was his name again? Dobson, that's right, and that woman....

"Sit down, Coral, and make yourself comfortable."

It was her! The woman with the jacket who came to see her dad all those years ago. Her hair was different, and she'd put on weight, but it was her. She'd looked very important with her clipboard and businesslike hairdo when Coral was a kid. Now she just looked like a bully.

"Now, Coral, do you know why you're here?" Mr Dobson began.

"I suppose it's about my next position."

"Well, that's true—in a way. You see, we must make a decision about what's best for you, and what's best for Rodney."

Coral nodded as they all looked over to the lady in the corner, bouncing Rodney on her knee. She'd stopped lemon sucking and had a broad smile on her face. "Isn't he just lovely?" she said, "Beautiful fair hair, and the most adorable blue eyes. We won't have a problem finding someone to.." her voice had trailed off to nothing before she cooed, "Oh he's just so lovely."

Coral smiled. She was secretly very proud when people admired her baby, then remembered what Mr Dobson had just said. "I'm sorry it didn't work out with the Murray's but I know my next position will be great. I'm learning new things all the time."

"While we understand that, Coral, you need to recognise our predicament. No employers are in want of a worker with a child. Surely you know yourself how difficult it is to tend to your baby and perform the required amount of work for a wage?"

"Yes, but I'd hoped—"

"We've made the decision to remove Rodney from your care, under the Infant Life Protection Provisions of the Child Welfare Act of 1922."

Mrs Dawson placed papers on the desk in front of Coral, but her mind was jumbled, flashing images and thoughts and her throat dried and constricted. "Life protec—Remove?" Coral's voice trailed off, but it was as if no one heard it at all, anyway.

"He will be placed with Miss Staines here, who runs a fine babies home in Werribee."

"But Werribee's miles away."

"You, of course, will be responsible for his upkeep using the wages from your next position. There's no reason you can't do well, Coral."

"I want to keep him with me." Coral tried to stop her tears but they exploded from within her, wrought by the terror flooding her veins. She held no weapon, no retaliation, no just cause, no bargaining chip. Nothing.

"How Coral? How can you provide for him?" Mrs Dawson asked.

Miss Staines stood holding Rodney in her arms. "Yes, how?" she demanded.

Mr Dobson went on and on about having no work, and feeding and clothing Rodney, and something about being under their guardianship and having no choice. Coral was only half listening. All she could concentrate on was Rose's voice in her head. *'They'll get him y'know.'*

"But he's mine, he's all I have, I'm all he has," she whispered, but no one heard at all.

Someone placed a pen in her hand. It didn't matter who it was.

"But if I find a position that will—"

Miss Staines appeared behind her and rested her hand on Coral's shoulder. Coral knew she was trying to comfort her, but her hand felt cold and lifeless. "Be a good mother now. You must think of poor Rodney."

Coral's heart beat roared through every nerve in her body and no matter how much she gasped she couldn't get enough air into her lungs. She clung onto the desk with wide eyes, convinced she was about to faint, or even die.

"Now, now." Mr Dawson said, "Enough with the theatrics... why do they always do this sort of thing?"

Mrs Dawson pried Coral's fingers from the desk and encouraged her to breathe slowly and gain control of herself. "Really Coral, this behaviour is not becoming at all," she tutted.

Coral's lungs opened to the air, and her shoulders slumped. Her tears mingled with the ink, blurring her signature as she signed with a shaky hand.

She had nothing now.

They'd taken it all.

Where's Mrs Shaw?
Does she know what's going on?
Will she help me?
Why doesn't she do something?

Mr Dobson gently pulled at the paper from under Coral's hand. "Miss Staines will get things in order and call for Rodney at the Maternity Home."

Coral sniffed. "When?"

"You'll be notified in due course."

Ascot Vale

1949

Thursday 24th February, 1949—
C.W.D. Flinders Street Railway Building

Dulcie Shaw raced through the offices of the Children's Welfare Department. It was a rather undignified scene, but there was no time to waste. She was out of breath by the time she reached the office she shared with John Oxford.

"John!" she called as she flung their door open only to find the space occupied by the Welfare Secretary Mr Dobson, a rather bemused Mrs Dawson, and a dark-haired woman she quickly assumed to be Miss Staines. *The Meeting*. "Oh, I'm terribly sorry Mr Dobson, I expected Mr Oxford to have returned by now."

"Not quite yet, as you can see. We'll be on our way then."

"Wait!" Dulcie's lack of oxygen also affected her manners. Mr Dobson raised his eyebrows, and Dulcie collected her thoughts. "I was going to contact you shortly, anyway. This saves us both a telephone call."

"Go ahead Mrs Shaw."

"Do you mind looking over this report?" Mrs Shaw fumbled through her briefcase and produced a folder. "It's about Coral Maxwell."

"Oh, you just missed her."

"I did? That's a shame. I have news for her."

Mr Dobson flipped through the pages of information and nodded his head. "So, you've found a place for the girl?"

"Mrs Gladys Hutchinson, as you can see there. She's a widow, an agent for Herbert Adams, and runs her own shop. She's most anxious to take Coral *and* her baby."

Miss Staines shifted so violently, Dulcie felt sure she'd stomped her foot on the ground. "We've already made plans for the child!"

Mrs Shaw's chest tightened, and she returned her attention to Mr Dobson. "The only condition is that Coral agrees to be known as *Mrs* Maxwell, for obvious reasons. Award wages of 2 pound, 12 shillings, and sixpence per week."

"It does sound like the good placement for the girl."

"Could we let Sister Kelly know, please? Coral's accommodation will be in the building and Mrs Hutchinson said she'd be delighted to have the child and considers it would be better for Coral and she will advise her in any way possible."

"Yes, yes, go ahead, Mrs Shaw." He handed the file back to her. "If you're happy with the finer details, you have my approval."

"Thank you, Mr Dobson, I'll get her wages book and agreement organised today."

Monday 28th February, 1949—Union Road, Ascot Vale

"Well, here she is." Gladys Hutchinson greeted Coral with a hug. It felt weird to be in a stranger's welcoming arms; ones as soft and fleshy as Mrs Hutchinson's, too. Must be all those cakes in the display cases they walked past to get to the living area at the back of the shop.

"I'll be off then." Sister Kelly patted Coral's shoulder and wished them well.

"Let me put the kettle on and we'll have a quick chat before they need me in the shop again. Tea?"

"Yes, please." Coral took a seat at the small dining table and jiggled Rodney on her lap.

"Oh, what a bonnie babe, young Coral. You must be so pleased with him."

"I am."

"So, they tell me you've got yourself into a predicament."

Coral kissed the top of Rodney's head. "You could say that."

Mrs Hutchinson looked from side to side as if she was about the share a secret and the kettle started a slow and deep whistle in response. "Other people can't choose things for you, particularly men in suits! Life pushes us all into corners and we have to decide the best way to go. Everyone told me to give up the shop; that I couldn't do it with two young girls, but I did. Mind you, they weren't babies. This will take some work, Coral, but we have to give it a go; a damn good go—agreed?"

Coral nodded and set her cup of tea out of Rodney's reach. "Agreed."

"Here," Mrs Hutchinson put a selection of cakes on the table. "Help yourself."

Coral chose a small slice of fruitcake and relaxed into the wooden chair. Mrs Hutchinson's lounge room wasn't large, just enough space for her lounge suite, a bookcase or two, and her dining table. A little corner kitchen and a refrigerator took up the rest of the floor, and the wireless had pride of place and its own special polished table near the window. She imagined the bedrooms were through the doors on the other side.

Mrs Hutchinson looked at Coral's suitcase near her feet. "Where are his things?"

"Things?"

"Like his pram, cot, and mattress?"

"They don't provide them."

"That's a bit rough then, isn't it?"

Coral shrugged and snatched a sip of tea while Rodney was distracted by the tablecloth.

"So, you're supposed to buy them?"

"I guess so. The other lady, Mrs Murray, already had those things, so I hadn't given it much thought."

Mrs Hutchinson chuckled. "I'm well beyond having those items in my house. Do you have the money to purchase them then?"

"I do, but the department holds all my money other than wages. For my savings."

"Alright then. You can telephone them and tell them you need some money."

"They won't let me have any without a guardian vouching for me."

"Ridiculous. You're an adult, aren't you?" Mrs Hutchinson devoured a cream bun and licked her fingers clean. "We could make this two-against-one. On the telephone, at least."

Coral's eyes were wide, and her mind a jumble.

Mrs Hutchinson patted her hand. "I'll call, then you call after me."

Coral's mouth was getting drier by the moment. While Rodney slept peacefully on the thick rug on Mrs Hutchinson's lounge room floor, they stepped into the small office between the shop and her home. Mrs Hutchinson picked up the phone stand and held the receiver to her ear.

"Mrs Shaw? I have Coral Maxwell with me. Yes, yes, she's settling in quite well, just getting to know each other over a cup of tea. Now Coral is in need of some equipment for the baby. Well, a cot and mattress for one, and a pram, I suppose."

Mrs Hutchinson checked with Coral, who nodded her approval.

"Yes, I expect anything else can come from her wages. It's just the expense of the larger items you see. Coral will telephone you shortly to make the request herself. Yes, thank you Mrs Shaw. Goodbye."

Mrs Hutchinson put the receiver in the cradle and ended her call. "Now you call them Coral."

Coral eyes widened until she thought they'd fall out of her head and her head trembled in a shake.

"You have to start doing things for yourself now. Show them you can make your own decisions and not just do what you're told. There's a wonderful woman under there. I know it. Time to grow up."

Coral's mouth felt like sandpaper. "Do I have to?"

"Do you need these items or not?"

"Yes. Rodney needs them."

"He's your baby Coral; time to be his mum."

Coral bit into the side of her lip. "But I don't know how to call them."

"Alright." Mrs Hutchinson patted the other chair in the office and pulled out a notepad. "Let's think things through and decide on what you need to say. It makes you sound more confident, and will make you feel more confident, too. Let's practice talking about what you want and how much you would like." She licked the end of her pencil. "First things first. Let's add up how much you'll need."

The ringing tone sounded louder than what Coral had imagined. The phone stand shook in her hand and the receiver was hard against her ear.

Janet answered. She'd know her voice anywhere, but kept to her practiced script.

"Hello, this is Coral Maxwell. May I speak with Mrs Shaw please?"

Coral's eyes landed on her shoes. "Yes, 6-6-4-2-0" she mumbled. "6-6-4-2-0" she repeated.

Her voice was shaky, and she didn't know where to look.

Would they say no?

Did they say 'yes' to Mrs Hutchinson?

Mrs Hutchinson gracefully lifted her hand from her chest to high above her head like a ballet dancer, and Coral remembered to stand tall.

"I'd like to access some of my savings please,"

Mrs Hutchinson nodded her encouragement.

"It's for some things for Rodney; essential things.... seventeen pounds, please." Coral smiled into the phone. "Thank you. May we collect a cheque tomorrow?"

Mrs Hutchinson smiled and nodded.

"We'll be there at..."

'Nine,' Mrs Hutchinson mouthed.

"We'll be there at nine. Thank you."

Coral put the phone down and let out a squeal of delight and relief.

"That's perfect Coral," Mrs Hutchinson was on her way back to the living room, "We can collect your cheque and cash it at the bank on Collins Street on our way to Myer. Later, we'll catch the tram home with Rodney in his new buggy. I'm sure they'll deliver his other things in the afternoon." Mrs Hutchinson stopped short in the middle of her lounge room and Coral nearly ran in to her. "But for tonight... hmm."

"I could keep him in bed with me."

"No, I won't have you sleeping with the baby. Have you heard what the doctors are saying? Anything could happen." Mrs Hutchinson watched Rodney sleep on the rug. "I'll find a box in the store and we can lay some towels down. It shouldn't be a problem for one night. We'll pop him on the dresser, so he's away from any draughts."

Mrs Hutchinson tip-toed into Coral's room. Coral was reading by lamp-light and smiled as she entered.

"I couldn't resist," Mrs Hutchinson said as she peered into the large box on Coral's dresser. Rodney was sound asleep.

Coral put her book down and leant forward to whisper, "He smells like chocolate scrolls."

"That's because he's such a delicious little boy."

Thursday 3rd March, 1949—Union Road, Ascot Vale

"Ready my love?"

Coral tucked a stray hair away in the hair net under her white cap. Her uniform was a white apron over a blue checked dress, and every day she learnt something new about the world of cakes, weighing scales, money, and people. She smiled into the mirror. She looked like a real shop girl.

Mrs Hutchinson looped her arm through Coral's as they crossed the living room. "There's only one thing I love more than cakes, Coral, and that's proving people wrong. Let's get to work!"

The shop floor was very simple. Three large glass cabinets in a U shape let the customers choose what they'd like to buy, and the girls behind the counters weighed and wrapped their choices. The best selections in the cabinet always faced the customers, but that didn't stop Coral admiring the dented cakes and pastries that faced her. She planned to try them all. The shortbreads, jam rolls, fruitcakes, and iced sponge cakes were all piled high on doily lined shelves behind her, and the cabinet overflowed with slices of butter rich cakes, cherry, chocolate, ginger, walnut, and every other cake imaginable. Mrs Hutchinson also sold fresh eggs from a basket on the counter.

Coral handed the awkwardly wrapped almond cake to her customer. It wasn't pretty, but it was better than her wrapping on the first day. Everything was getting better, even the cash register didn't seem so scary now.

One of the shop girls tapped her on the shoulder and whispered, "Coral, it's Rodney," and stepped in to serve. All the girls kept an ear out for him, and Mrs Hutchinson docked her time with him as her lunch break.

"Don't forget to eat," Mrs Hutchinson called from the office as she passed.

When Coral returned to the store, Mrs Hutchinson was talking to another lady, where there was a gap in the counters. "Coral, over here," she waved.

"I'd like to introduce you to one of my daughters. Lorna, this is Coral, Coral, Lorna,"

"Pleased to meet you," they said in unison.

Lorna was taller than Mrs Hutchinson, and quite a bit thinner. She seemed very proper, like a schoolteacher, or perhaps a minister's wife.

"Remember when I said there was only one thing I loved more than cakes? You'd better make that two."

"Did you forget me again, Mum?" Lorna laughed. "You best make that three before Irene finds out you've been making that joke again."

Lorna smiled at Coral, "She forgot me again, didn't she?" and Coral nodded. "You must come for tea, Coral, and bring your little boy. I can't wait to meet him."

"Thank you, we will."

Mrs Hutchinson leant her head towards Coral. "Lorna lives on Roseberry Street, just a little way down the road. I often pop in for a cuppa when I need time away from the shop."

"Well, that's it for me, Mum. One more stop at the butcher and then home to the garden." Lorna collected her basket, and with a ding of the doorbell, she was gone.

Mrs Hutchinson gave Coral a wink. "Back to work now, love."

Coral worked hard all day. When she wasn't serving customers, she was cleaning or restocking the shelves. There was hardly a minute to catch her breath, but she didn't worry because she knew there was an entire shop full of people listening out for Rodney.

Coral leant into the cabinet so far she thought she might fall in. Cleaning the inside of the glass window was a stretch, and now she just had to reattach the stars and ribbons that announced the specials. *'Ding!'* The courier from the Postmaster General looked all wonky through the glass, and Coral didn't feel like clambering to her feet again. Thank goodness he wasn't a customer and that Mrs Hutchinson received the telegram and he was on his way again. *'Ding'* All she needed to do now was secure that last wretched star and she'd be done.

Mrs Hutchinson disappeared into her office and appeared a few minutes later. She mustn't have noticed Coral's half body sticking out of the cabinet. "Vera, can you come in tomorrow? I know it's your day off, but Coral won't be in."

Coral won't be in. She knew she had inadvertently overheard a conversation not meant for her. Should she bring it up? Perhaps Mrs Hutchinson would tell her later. Was it a surprise? Perhaps they're going shopping again. Coral made sure she gave the glass an extra polish.

Mrs Hutchinson let out a long-held breath. "Whew, what a day."

Coral had already made them each a cup of tea and looked at her watch. "Rodney should be up soon."

Surprisingly, Mrs Hutchinson turned the oven off, pulled the telegram from her pocket, and nodded to the kitchen table.

"Coral, my love. Sit down."

Friday 4th March, 1949—Roseberry Street, Ascot Vale

It was quiet in Lorna's sitting room, just her and Rodney breathing alone. He'd always been there. She'd always been there. Every night, every morning, every day. Relying on each other.

Mrs Hutchinson had telephoned and organised the collection from there. Coral wouldn't have thought of that. There'd be so much noise in the shop, so many people watching and asking questions.

Coral groaned inwardly. Why did she sign that stupid piece of paper at the Welfare Office? And why did that horrible Staines woman insist it be honoured?

Rodney wiped at his nose in his sleep. His cold had just about cleared up, and he only had a tiny little snuffle snore left. His little nose, little hands, and gurgles were supposed to be part of something that couldn't be taken away. *Family*. But she had been wrong again.

Remember, it's only for a little while.

Mrs Hutchinson said they would work it out and get Rodney home again, but that they couldn't do it right now. Not this minute. Not with Miss Staines about to turn up on the doorstep and...

Coral's jaw tightened. She did everything they asked! Why this? They're demanding him, like they own him, but they don't!

"The car's here."

It was a gentle warning, but it punched deep into her chest. There wasn't enough air in the world to help expand her lungs. She'd stared at his face all morning, remembering every dimple, every eyelash.

It's only for a little while.

Rodney was oblivious, rugged up in his favourite blanket as Coral carried him to the small front garden. A tall man in a suit held the gate open for Miss Staines. Coral's teeth clenched; that Staines woman and her pinched mouth weren't to step any further into her life than this garden. *Futile.* It was a word she'd heard but never understood until now.

Miss Staines hands were cold. She could feel their iciness through the woman's gloves as they slipped under Rodney and pulled him from her arms. A gasp caught in her throat, held in place by the unimaginable scene in front of her.

The tall man hustled them to the car, strode around to the driver's side, and dipped his hat.

Coral knew she was supposed to smile at his nicety but couldn't.

Mrs Hutchinson appeared by her side. She'd said to be brave, like all the wives waving their husbands off to war. It'd only be a short while that she'd have to stand there and control herself. Breaking down would only make things worse. Coral had agreed; the last thing she wanted was *'hysterical'* written across her file.

Coral agreed then, but she didn't know how impossible it would be to remain calm.

Mrs Hutchinson also said they'd win.

But this didn't feel anything like winning.

'Coral, my love, this will be hard. Don't forget to breathe deeply.' Coral couldn't even do that. Her body forgot how to breathe and clung to the moment as if it was the only one that existed.

Anguish flared to life deep within Coral's belly the moment Miss Staines prised Rodney from her arms. It swept to her chest, stinging and scorching as the woman sat smugly in the car, then rose further with the doff of the man's hat and the slam of the car door.

The engine growled and Coral was sure she'd never breathe again. Invisible hands formed around her throat and squeezed, compressing the pain until she thought her chest would burst into a million pieces.

'Rose was right,' Coral tried to speak, but the invisible hands made sure she stayed lifeless and mute. *'They take a piece of your heart. Scoop it out, so*

all you feel is hollow. And then you find you're doing things you said you'd never do, ever. Things you promised to yourself and to your baby.

Like saying goodbye.

Like sending them away.

How is it possible I'm doing the one thing I said I'd never do in my life?'

Mrs Hutchinson caught her as she fell.

"I'm so proud of you, Coral," she whispered. "Grieve all you need. They can't see you now."

Monday 7th March, 1949—
C.W.D. Flinders Street Railway Building

"Letter from Mrs Murray."

"Murray? Sorry Mr Oxford, all these new cases have me spinning me in circles—"

"Mrs Murray from Nhill. She has a few questions for us?"

"What questions would she have for us? Coral's no longer employed there."

Dear Sir,

I trust you will pardon me for troubling you again, but as we have not heard anything from Coral Maxwell since the day she left here, I would be grateful if you will let me know where she is (if you think it advisable) and whether she has the baby or not. We did not want her to feel that she had lost friends because we could not keep her as we had really thought we could do. She had promised to write and we really are wondering how the poor child is, so if you would be kind enough, we would be grateful to have her address. I also have a coat and a frock here belonging to her.

Yours Faithfully,
Mrs. H. E. Murray

Friday 11th March, 1949—
C.W.D. Flinders Street Railway Building

Mrs Shaw picked up her handbag and left the office, then popped her head back in. "Have you replied to Mrs Murray yet? She's always very quick to reply and might start sending us telegrams if we're not quick enough."

Mr Oxford pulled paper from his desk drawer. "Doing it now."

Dear Mrs Murray,
With reference to your letter of the 7th instant, I have to advise that the above-named ward and her child are now placed with Mrs. G Hutchinson, of Union Road, Ascot Vale.

Monday 21st March, 1949—Union Road, Ascot Vale

Coral sat on the back steps of the cake shop. Mrs Hutchinson's backyard wasn't really a garden, more like a patch of short grass with a red leaved plum tree that hung over the paling fence and into the alley behind it. Coral loved being here; away from the shop, the trams and the busyness of Union Road on a Monday afternoon. Mrs Hutchinson hummed in the washroom, but Coral didn't feel much like humming or doing anything.

"Up you get." Mrs Hutchinson's warning sent Coral plodding down the stairs and out of the way of her washing basket. "Get the line for me, love."

Coral lifted the timber pole that held the washing line high and let it lean where it sat.

"Feeling like a chat today?"

Coral shook her head. It was the same question Mrs Hutchinson asked every day. She didn't force her to talk about it, or tell her to not to think about Rodney. She just enquired after her every day and only asked her to wear a smile in the shop.

Coral picked some clothes from the washing basket and pegged them on the line. She wanted to talk. She wanted to get all the feelings and thoughts out of her body, but they were so tangled she didn't know where to start. She stomped on a dandelion that dared to poke its head from under the washing basket and twisted it into the ground with her foot. Coral clenched her fists, and they trembled in anger. "I hate her!"

Mrs Hutchinson nodded and kept pegging.

"I hate her so much! I wanted to scream and wrench Rodney back from her. That awful, awful... bitch! But I just stood there! I stood there like an idiot, stuck solid on the front lawn. Who would do such a thing?" Coral's tears were hot, fuelled by the emotion spilling out of her. She'd collapsed, screamed, and cried for days when she took him, but just when she felt stable, another wave of emotions would crash over her. She never knew what was coming. Sometimes it was incredible sadness, or rage, then disdain would come and she'd develop a deep hatred for herself. They all tangled among the threads of propriety, and duty, self-consciousness about her fate. Mrs Hutchinson had been patient with her outbursts, but Coral felt different now, like she was going round and round in circles and it would never stop.

Mrs Hutchinson put her hand on her hip. "Who would do such a thing? A mother without a choice in the world. I'm so sorry this happened to you, my love."

Coral fell into her arms and cried again. "My God, will these bloody tears ever stop?"

"They will. In their own time."

The clothes on the line waved in the soft breeze.

"There you are." Mrs Hutchinson handed Coral a cup of tea on her favourite back step. Mrs Hutchinson landed somewhat awkwardly a couple of steps behind her and spilt some of her tea. "Bugger. I'm going to need some help to get back up, I think. You like this spot, don't you?"

"There's not much to see."

"There's my plum tree, and some goings on in the lane, I suppose."

"Deliveries and people tripping over the bluestones, usually."

Mrs Hutchinson looked into her neighbours' yards. "It's quieter than the front. To think, I had this quiet space here all along and I never used it."

A delivery truck bumped its way along the laneway. The sign on the side said *McAlpins Flour*. They both know it's headed to the bakery, so there was no point mentioning it.

Mrs Hutchinson sighed and put her cup down. "What do you want, Coral?"

Coral fished for words. "What do you mean, what do I want?"

"What do you want from life? When you look forward—years into the future—what do you see?"

Coral felt her cheeks redden. "I don't know," she paused. "Nobody's ever asked me that before."

"Well, I'm asking you now. I'd like to know. What do you want from your life?"

Tears pricked Coral's eyes. "Nothing much."

"What about if you dream?"

"Dream?" The idea of a dream hurt Coral's chest, and she moved her palm there to soften the pain.

"I know you don't want to hear this, but you have to make some decisions. Just like I did when my husband died. These moments come along and define who we are. Only, by the looks of you, everyone's just told you what to do, and you've just simply done it."

"I try to be a good girl, I do, but it never seems to work out for me."

"Stuff being a good girl!"

Coral jumped on the step and turned to look at Mrs Hutchinson. Did she hear right?

"You're 19 now, aren't you? Not quite an adult by some standards, but you have to start thinking for yourself. Taking control. Look where the 'good girl' thing landed you. Lord knows the department doesn't care about how practical their teaching is; you didn't even know how to make a polite phone call, or access your own money. What on earth are they preparing you for?"

Coral had never thought about it that way. She was so busy concentrating on being a good girl and doing the right things she had no thoughts about her future. None at all. So, it didn't matter what happened with her life, because it was never really hers to begin with. What did she want? She didn't know. She frowned as Mrs Hutchinson continued.

"You have to be your own person, not an extension of someone else's idea of who you should be. So again, Coral, what do you want? Do you want to run a cake shop like me? Be a business owner? The world is changing, the 50s are just around the corner. Where will you be? What will you do? Imagine yourself all peaceful and content. Go on, do it. Close your eyes if it helps. C'mon, surely you've dreamed of what your future might look like?"

"It's stupid."

"Come on. Close your eyes. Can you see yourself?"

Coral sighed and tried to imagine herself in the future. At first, she was just all flustered and angry about having to do this exercise to keep Mrs Hutchinson happy. Then she calmed a little and wondered what the years might bring her. It took a while for her body to settle, and for a small smile to stretch her lips. "Yes, I can see myself."

"How does it feel?"

"I'm happy, and relaxed, and I'm smiling."

"That sounds lovely. Who's there with you?"

A tear slid down Coral's cheek. "Rodney."

"Where are you? At a shop, on a farm?"

"A house."

"Are you by yourself?"

"No. I have my own family."

"How delightful Coral. And you're filled with joy? You want for nothing else?"

Coral kept her eyes closed and tipped her face to the sky. "Nothing at all. It's perfect."

"Then we must chase your dream!"

Coral's vision popped like a bubble in the sky, and the sinking feeling returned to her chest. "Dreams and wishes don't work. We used to wish on dandelions at the girls' home, but nothing ever came of my wishes. I'm no good at it."

"Nonsense. Let's try again. Nothing like a bit of whimsy to brighten your day."

"What's the point?" she sighed, but Mrs Hutchinson was already on her feet and pushing her way past Coral. It was too squeezy, and Coral ended up at the bottoms of the steps, whether she wanted to be there or not.

"Help me look. There's got to be one here somewhere."

Mrs Hutchinson hunted earnestly for a dandelion. Behind the bins, along the fences, and under the stairs, while Coral shook her head and swept her gaze across the whole of the yard.

You'd think Mrs Hutchinson had struck gold when she found a lopsided stalk growing along her fence line in the alley. She rushed it to Coral and held it up to her face. "Go on. Blow on it, make a wish."

The stalk was bent and half its head had been pushed in as it grew along the fence. "No thanks," Coral whispered. "I've given up on wishing and hoping."

"Ah, but you see, this time there's a difference. We're going to make a plan. Something you could never do before. We don't just make a wish and do nothing; we wish and act upon it. It's called intention. Has anyone explained that to you before?"

"No, I just thought you wished and if you were lucky enough, it came true."

"Ah, no my love. I'll show you how it works. We'll make an intention about what you're going to do, and how we expect it to work out. The wish is more like a ritual, like a promise you're making to yourself."

"Can I make the promise to Rodney instead of myself?"

"Of course you can! What matters is following it up with action." Mrs Hutchinson held the floppy dandelion in front of Coral's face. "So, make your wish, and let's get to work."

Coral wasn't sure where her breath came from. She felt like she hadn't breathed properly for weeks, but it blew every one of those seeds off into the gentle breeze to work their magic.

Mrs Hutchinson set their dinner plates on the kitchen table. It had been another long afternoon and now that the day had settled, they could return to their earlier conversation. They'd normally start their dinner talking about the meal, the price of the lamb chops, how fresh the beans were, and how quickly the potatoes got peeled and dropped into the pot. But that night was different. That night was about making plans.

"Mmm." Mrs Hutchinson took a moment to appreciate her lamb chop. "Have you ever made plans before, Coral?"

"Not really. I've never had to."

"I don't expect they'd want you girls to go making your own plans."

"But I've thought about it, and I've come up with my own plan!"

"You have?" Mrs Hutchinson set aside her cutlery and leant towards Coral with a smile. "Tell me all about it."

"Well. Seeing as the department has made it perfectly clear that I can't fight them and their decisions, this is what I'm going to do."

Mrs Hutchinson nodded along.

"When I get my next wage, I'll go down to Werribee and I'll take him back!"

"Ahh, then what will you do? How will you feed him and yourself? Where will you sleep?" Mrs Hutchinson rubbed at her chin. "And what do you think they'll do when they find you? And they will. Too many people make up their minds about young girls with babies before they know any part of the story."

Coral knew what she said was true and slumped her head onto her hand and pushed her beans around the plate.

"Your plan was good." Mrs Hutchinson began, "It was all about getting Rodney back with you. But we have to find a way we don't aggravate them and make the situation worse. We can't give them any opportunity to say you can *never* have Rodney back."

Coral was aghast. "They can't do that. I did nothing wrong."

"Oh, they can; and they will, if you give them any cause." Mrs Hutchinson picked up her cutlery and thoughtfully collected a few beans and a slice of potato on her fork. "When's your first visit?"

"This weekend."

"Right. Werribee is 45 miles away. Tomorrow, go to the train station and ask for the Geelong line timetable. Know the time of every train. And always catch the first one in case something goes wrong."

Coral nodded. Plans made her feel more whole. Less scattered.

Mrs Hutchinson pointed her fork at Coral. "Will you miss a train?"

Coral didn't break eye contact. "Never!"

"Good girl." Mrs Hutchinson cut some more of her meat, but stopped before eating it. "You're responsible for his upkeep. Will you miss a payment?"

"But you do my wages—oh! Never!"

Mrs Hutchinson gobbled up her cut meat and was cutting her vegetables faster than she could devour them. "We shall beat them at their own game, Coral! Save your money, perhaps one day get a flat, and bring Rodney home to you once you're settled. Some dreams you can't have just now. Sometimes you have to be patient and wait a little longer."

"Dreams *and* plans."

"Mmm- mm", Mrs Hutchinson nodded with a mouth full of potato and lifted her glass. "To dreams and plans."

Coral copied her enthusiasm. "To dreams and plans,"

Their glasses clinked, and Mrs Hutchinson added, "and a little bit of *bugger off.*"

Thursday 21st April, 1949—Union Road, Ascot Vale

Coral stretched herself awake and watched the grey cloud drift like a damp sheet across her window. Mornings were weird, a daily reminder of the contradiction of her life. She was rested; she was sleeping better now, but the reason she was so rested was that Rodney wasn't with her. Her comfort reminded her of the cost to her heart.

The shop kept her busy, and she found it worked to her advantage. She knew any thoughts of whether Rodney was crying or cold or needed her were drowned by customer requests and the vital importance of the shop being swept. The accusing voices, the ones that reminded her she did what she said she'd never do, they came when it was quiet, at night-time when she couldn't find anything to do.

"Coral, Coral. Oh, there you are. Honestly, child, you're going to sweep the colour out of that lino if you keep going."

Coral collected the dustpan to capture the miniscule amount of dust she'd swept up.

"You really need to get out. Don't you have any friends in the area?"

"I bumped into Allison last week. She was in a line for the pictures."

"Well, there you go."

"She lives in Richmond now."

"That's not too far away. Why not contact her and meet up at the pictures sometime? You can't simply work, visit Rodney, and then mope about the house in your spare time. It's not healthy for a young girl like you."

Friday 29th April, 1949—Union Road, Ascot Vale

Coral grabbed her gloves and headed to the front door. She stopped to place a kiss on top of Mrs Hutchinson's head. "I'm meeting Allison at the pictures."

"Again? What are you seeing this time?"

"Mr Blandings Builds His Dream House."

"A comedy will do you good. And looking at Cary Grant won't hurt either."

Coral laughed. "Just for my eyes, though. Allison's husband, Alex, is working late again, so we're catching the early screening at Richmond." She was almost at the door when Mrs Hutchinson called to her over her shoulder. "Don't waste your money on sweeties."

"No fear. Money to see Rodney gets tucked away in the special section of my purse. I only spend what's in this part."

"Very clever, my love, don't give them any reason or opportunity to say you don't want him or aren't interested in visiting him. I have to write to them soon with your wages. How about I add a letter with a few suggestions of my own?"

Coral stopped putting her gloves on.

"You will?"

"Absolutely. First off, let's get him moved closer to you. How ridiculous to have him all the way down in Werribee."

"Really? You can ask for that?"

"I'm going to try. Now off with you, or you'll miss the newsreel."

<u>Saturday 30th April, 1949—Union Road, Ascot Vale</u>

Coral clamped her hand down on her hat. Those northerlies were gusting well before their time. *Quick! Quick!.* Her shoes clacked their way along the footpath. Only now she wished she hadn't stopped to admire the new season's dresses in the window. She could hear the train gathering steam. The engineer was testing the pressure and preparing the Geelong train for departure. Coral checked her watch. She had time, but only just.

"One ticket to Werribee please," she asked at the window.

The station master slid the paper stub under the ornate grill, but experience kept his fingertips in place until after the transaction had taken place. "That'll be four shillings, love."

"Yes, that's right." Coral answered. She just needed to get her ticket and seat herself on the train, for this panic to be over.

She panicked every time. This time was worse, of course, but that was all her own fault, anyway. She rummaged about in her handbag; her purse wasn't in its usual place. Must've put it somewhere different among all the commotion at the pictures last night. The pictures! No matter how many times she swung her hand around inside her handbag, the purse just wasn't there.

"Do you want the ticket or not?"

"Yes, I..." Inside her chest, a heavy load landed inside her heart and threatened to drag it to her feet. The implications of the moment rolled around in her head, and she gasped at the air but couldn't catch her breath.

The stationmaster rolled his eyes and removed the ticket. Suddenly Coral felt cold and exposed and alone. Dizzy now, she reached for the wall to steady her as she sucked in the unfulfilling air. The train built up its steam, and she didn't know whether she was about to cry, vomit, or faint.

Allison's muffled voice felt like a weird hallucination. "Look, it's Coral. Hey Coral!" Allison walked between two men, coming from the other platform. She laughed out loud. "Fancy meeting you here! I talked Alex and Bill into looking at that pretty sideboard at Anderson's, didn't expect to see—" Allison's mirth and face drained when she noticed Coral's predicament.

"Coral, what's wrong?"

"My purse... gone."

The train whistle blew, and Coral groaned. Those invisible hands were coming for her throat again.

"Money!" Allison shouted at the men. "Who's got money?"

The men pulled out wallets and emptied pockets.

"You!" she shouted to the stationmaster. "What ticket did she want?"

"Werribee."

The men slapped money onto the counter and Allison grabbed the ticket just as the train whistle blew.

"All aboard," they heard from behind the station gates.

"Go Coral," Allison shouted, "Run!"

Coral pulled the sash window down in her compartment and waved through the engine's steam at the three bodies behind the platform's iron gate. She'd made it.

What was that other man's name again? *Bill*. She must remember to thank him.

Saturday 14th May, 1949—Union Road, Ascot Vale

Coral thought about using the cake shop's wrapping paper for the gift, but lashed out and bought some colourful paper at the general store. She clasped it as she wound the string around the parcel, but she couldn't get it just right, and she left it all come apart again on the kitchen table. The wrapping paper was getting more crumpled each time, and she was getting frustrated.

Mrs Hutchinson shuffled into the living room with her chenille robe dragging across the carpet. "You're up extra early."

"I can't miss anything today," she smiled. "It's Rodney's birthday tomorrow, so I'm taking his gift on my visiting day today." The crumpled paper reminded her how the more she tried, the more it got messed up. She sighed deeply. "This isn't at all how I expected to celebrate his first birthday."

"I know, love. But there will be many more to make up for it."

"That's what Bill said, and that Rodney probably won't even remember this one."

"That's true. Ah, so you bought the gift? Let me see."

Mrs Hutchinson admired the wooden duck pull toy. "Oh, that's lovely, Coral. He'll be pulling that all over the place before you know it."

Coral pulled it across the table, "See how it makes that clack sound? It almost sounds like 'quack'. Bill said it should be colourful to keep Rodney's interest."

"Oh, I agree, what baby wouldn't love this? He's almost walking now, isn't he?"

"Almost. He tries but falls down. Bill said it would encourage his walking, too."

"Hmm, it seems this Bill has a lot to say." Mrs Hutchinson lit the stove for the kettle. "When will I be meeting this mystery, Bill?"

"He's not really a mystery. He's Allison's brother-in-law."

"And he knows about Rodney?"

Coral nodded. "He often comes down to Werribee with me. Except for when he has to work. Then he insists his brother escort me. He said he's worried about the characters that catch the train to the Werribee Races, and doesn't like to see me travelling alone."

"That seems like a very kind offer."

"Yes, it does, doesn't it?"

INSPECTOR'S REPORT
Tuesday 17th May, 1949—
Miss Staines's Home for Babies, Werribee

RODNEY MAXWELL (15.05.1948)

A nice fair child, has made good progress, and is well cared for. Dr Purcell doing his rounds of the children at the time of my visit.

Tuesday 24th May, 1949—
C.W.D. Flinders Street Railway Building

"Goodness, it's *pig money*!" Mrs Shaw giggled.

"It's what?" Mr Oxford took the letter from Dulcie Shaw's hand and read it himself and chuckled. "How unexpected, and simply... delightful!"

Dear Sir,
We have here a cheque for the sum of 5 pound, 2 shillings, and 5 pence for Coral Maxwell; it is the balance of some pig money or rather the pigs were sold for her after she left here and as we have only heard from Coral once since she left us, we wondered whether she is still at Ascot Vale and so think it wiser to send to it to you to bank it for her. Trusting this will be satisfactory.
Yours Faithfully,
Mrs. H. E. Murray

Mr Oxford prepared the deposit details for the bank. "Well, I think that's the first time I've been asked to add pig money to someone's savings. And to think they still honoured Coral's work and still sent it. Families like the Murrays are few and far between."

INSPECTOR'S REPORT
Friday 5th August, 1949—
C.W.D. Railway Buildings, Flinders Street

Inquired at the cake shop re Mrs Hutchinson and was directed to her daughter's home near to the shop. Mrs Hutchinson confirmed Coral was working in the shop and had complete charge of it during the mornings. Can be trusted with money, and is clean and tidy. Coral is a good worker but must be reminded what to do every day.

Mrs Hutchinson has been regularly paying the girl's savings to the department and also for Rodney Maxwell's board, which is deducted from Coral's weekly wage. Coral's child is placed with Miss Staines at Werribee, paying 15 shillings per week

Coral has been friendly with an Allison King of Richmond, and is very friendly with her brother-in-law, Bill King.
He calls at the home for Coral and takes her to the pictures and appears respectable. Is interested in her and has visited her child with her at Werribee.
Mrs Hutchinson is very satisfied with Coral.
Did not speak to Coral as she was on her own at the shop.

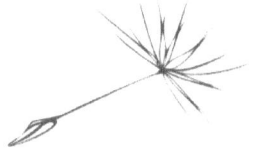

Saturday 6th August, 1949—Union Road, Ascot Vale

"It's so good to see you smiling again, love," Mrs Hutchinson placed two cups of tea on the kitchen table, with a slice of toast hanging out of her mouth. "Mmm," she said once she sat, "That new plum jam is quite nice. You having some this morning?"

"I think I will." Coral pulled the side of the toaster open to see how her toast was coming along. "Almost."

"The inspector that came to see me yesterday said he'd stopped in at the shop first."

"He did. So, I sent him to you at Lorna's."

"He found me, don't worry. Were you alright?"

"The inspectors always scare me. It's like they can decide anything for you, and you don't get a say. I worry each time they'll say I can't have Rodney back, or that I'll say something wrong."

"Don't you worry. I gave him what for. I said to him, 'So Coral was at the shop, running it herself, you say? Quite odd behaviour, for a girl you've labelled as handicapped and sub-normal don't you think?' and then when he got all flustered and tried to make excuses, I told him in no uncertain terms the department needs to stop labelling these girls." She laughed out loud. "I expect he's not used to back chat from a lady who loves her cakes!"

Coral laughed too and bit into her toast. Mrs Hutchinson was right. This new jam was delicious, but it didn't compete with the sweet feeling in her tummy that someone had taken the time to stand up for her. It felt wonderful, like she had more strength in her back or something.

"Bill going with you to Werribee today?"

"Alex unfortunately, not that it's not nice to have the company. It just seems a more pleasant trip when I'm with Bill."

"I understand."

"I'll be home later than usual, too. We're all going out for dinner when we get back."

"Righto."

Saturday 6th August, 1949—Union Hotel, Ascot Vale

The Union Hotel was busy, and apart from the occasional revelry from jubilant Footscray supporters, wasn't too noisy. The group found themselves a table for four in the lounge and considered the blackboard above the bar for the day's specials. A punter passed them, carrying his plate of roast, and Alex's nose followed along. "Grub doesn't look too bad here."

Bill stood, "Shandy?"[1] he asked Coral, and she nodded.

"The usual, love?" Alex said to Allison and was already on his way to the bar.

It was noisier at the bar, and Alex had to speak up to get Bill's attention. "Glad I got you alone. That's a shit place down at Werribee."

"It's just until she's on her feet."

"No, I don't mean anything about Coral. It's the way they run the place. It's dodgy."

It was Bill's turn to order, but he waved another man in. "What do you mean?"

"You've seen those pins, right?"

"You mean like nappy pins?"

"Yeah, but bigger and they're on the babies' clothes."

"Rodney's always dressed all right when we go down there."

---

1. A mixed drink of beer and lemonade

"That's 'cause you're visiting. I'm telling ya, you need to look at the other kids."

"What about them? What's all this about pins?"

Alex led Bill further away from the shouts at the bar. "You've seen the kids with their pyjamas tops on backwards?"

"Yeah, I just thought–"

"They pin them to the bed, mate. With their tops on backwards so they can't escape. Or even bloody move, for that matter."

"Shit!"

"And another thing," Alex checked around for eavesdroppers, "There's talk places like that *sell* some of the babies."

"Sell them?"

"They call it 'baby farming' and look, we both know Rodney's a good looking kid." Alex shook his head not quite believing his own words. "Should we tell Coral?"

"No. No. God, no. Nothing good'll come of it. It'll break her heart."

"Just thought you'd better know."

"Yeah, thanks, mate. And not a word to Coral."

Alex closed an imaginary zip across his lips, and they stepped back to the bar to order.

Coral ever so gently clicked the back door shut.

She inhaled as quietly as she could and turned as the lounge light flicked on and momentarily blinded her.

"Coral! What on earth do you think you're doing?"

"Am I late? Sorry I–"

"You're not late, you're just stupid! A stupid, stupid girl!"

Coral's eyes adjusted to the light and Mrs Hutchinson's temper. She'd never seen her so angry before.

"What do you call that carry on under the streetlight out there?"

"You were watching us?"

"I'm glad I did! All that... that... canoodling!"

"We were just kissing."

"And the rest! His hands looked quite comfortable resting in those other places."

"Mrs Hutchinson!"

"Don't you dare forget the real reason we are working so hard, missy!" Mrs Hutchinson wagged her finger at Coral, but her voice broke and tears formed as she squeaked out the last of her request. "You get yourself in trouble again. What will the department say about you? What will happen to Rodney?"

Coral burst into tears. "I didn't forget, I didn't. I just–"

Mrs Hutchinson took her in her arms. "I know, love. I know. But now is not the time for taking any chances. Agreed?"

Coral's head bobbed against her shoulder.

INSPECTOR'S REPORT
Tuesday 9th August, 1949—
Miss Staines's Home for Babies, Werribee

RODNEY MAXWELL (15.05.1948)

Miss Staines stated, when speaking on another matter, that as the mother of the child was only paying 15 shillings per week and was visiting the child with many male friends, Miss Staines has decided the child should be removed from the mother's care completely.

Efforts being made to effect this.

INSPECTOR'S REPORT
Monday 15th August, 1949—
C.W.D. Flinders Street Railway Building

Interviewed Coral today. Girl is happy, but an immature type, better than she was, having responsibility in the shop has helped her to a degree.

The boyfriend, Bill King, is a brother-in-law of her friend Allison King.

He is wanting to get a job as a driver with the West End Dry Cleaning firm.

Girl has not any plans for her child's future, but it would help considerably if the baby could be in Melbourne. The expense of travelling would be saved.

It is my firm opinion that Coral's term of guardianship should be extended for her own sake and the child's.

INSPECTOR'S REPORT
Tuesday 16th August, 1949—
Miss Staines's Home for Babies, Werribee

RODNEY MAXWELL (15.05.1948)

Rodney is a small fair child and is well.
Miss Staines says mother visits regularly accompanied by various male acquaintances.

Saturday 3rd September, 1949—Union Road, Ascot Vale

Mrs Hutchinson stepped gingerly from the kerb. The post box was just across the road. *Just across the road* for most, but she only noticed the two sets of tram tracks, four lanes of bitumen, the pothole on her left, and the road's slight lean to the right. Gaps in the early afternoon traffic gave her enough time to cross, but not without a cost to her hips, knees, and ankles. Must be all those years of up and down counter service. That's what the doctor suggested, anyway. She'd penned her letter yesterday, but needed to get it into the post box as soon as she could. She kissed the letter and prayed the department would view it favourably.

Dear Sir,
Enclosed please find cheque for Coral Maxwell's savings and Rodney Maxwell's board. As I am going to have a few months' rest from business, I am taking Coral with me to Roseberry St, Ascot Vale and if it meets with your approval, I will try and get her another position whilst she stays with me.

Yours Faithfully,
Mrs G M Hutchinson.

Saturday 10th September, 1949—
Miss Staines's Home for Babies, Werribee

Coral closed the low gate and looked back at the home on Synott Street. Leaving was harder each time.

"I don't know why that woman hates me," she said. "I haven't done anything to her."

Bill checked his watch. Twenty minutes until the last train to Melbourne left, and they had a twenty-minute walk ahead of them. "Maybe she's just one of those spinsters who gets old and bitter. C'mon now, love."

Coral dutifully stepped her woeful path back to the train, comforted by Bill's arm. "Did you see the way she sneered at me today? She's got it in for me. I know it."

"You alright? You seem a bit testy today. Being at Lorna's hasn't upset you?"

"The move was fine. It's quite nice living in a house instead of a shop, actually."

The train gathered steam and hissed and puffed its way from the station. They'd made it with a few minutes to spare. Coral kept to her usual habit, window down regardless of the weather, and waving goodbye in Rodney's direction. To complete her ritual, she would say, "Seven days until we meet again," and then land on the springy bench seat of her compartment.

Only then could Bill speak. He'd learnt the hard way.

Coral usually accepted this leg of the journey. The one that sent her back to Melbourne and her weekday life, but this time she was uneasy. She twisted her handkerchief until her hands went white.

"There, there, love," Bill soothed. "You'll be fine."

"No, I won't. There's something going on, something strange, but I don't know what. They'll find something. Something to blame me for. Did you hear a Geelong train came off the tracks last week?"

"Coral love, it was going too fast, they said–"

"What if it was my train? What if I was delayed and couldn't make it? They'd take him."

"Relax. You're worrying about something that hasn't even happened."

"But something *is* going on, Bill. You believe me, don't you?"

Bill nodded. There was no way he'd tell her about the pins on their pyjamas now.

"I want to move him out of there."

"Will they let you?"

"I don't know anymore. It feels like they make up new rules all the time."

Paddocks and bush passed by their window and the constant click clack of the wheels rocked them into a comfortable rest in the afternoon sun. Neither slept, but were kept awake by their thoughts and dilemmas.

Bill interrupted the relative silence. "Was there ever once, one particular drama or inconvenience, or a moment that you thought all of this wasn't worth it?"

"I imagine it might be for some people. But not me, not ever. Rodney will always be worth whatever they tell me to do." Once she'd answered, her teeth clenched. How dare he even think she'd consider such a thing, let alone say it? What an asshole.

"I just wanted to hear it from your mouth."

More silence.

Coral glared at him. She had more important things to think about than wonder why she ever liked this man in the first place.

After some time had passed, Bill cleared his throat. "Have you given any more thought to how you might get Rodney moved?"

Coral folded her arms. "I'll ask Mrs Hutchinson when we get back. She might know of a way."

Clickety clack. Clickety clack.

Trees passed by and the setting sun made pretty colours on the clouds. They would've impressed Coral more if she wasn't in such a bad mood.

Bill leant forward from his side of the compartment and rested his forearms on his knees. "I know of a way."

Coral looked up as a jostle of a track switch pushed Bill to the knees on the carriage floor.

"Are you alright?"

Bill opened his mouth to speak, and the train whistle blew its long warning at a level crossing. He tried again once they were clear. "Marry me! You're the girl I need by my side. You won't give up on Rodney, and you won't give up on me, and heavens knows I won't give up on you. That's a given."

The moment wasn't as happy as what Coral had imagined. In fact, what she thought would be an answer to all her problems suddenly flipped more feelings out of her system and sent them pouring out of her mouth.

"But they leave!" she blurted.

"Huh? I was kind of hoping for a 'yes'."

"They all leave. Everyone that ever said they cared. They left!" Coral's voice raised higher. She was louder than the train tracks, and she didn't care. My dad said he'd come back, and he didn't. Mr Reynolds died, Matron Bradbury died, you'd think being kind to me was some kind of death sentence. The Hughes' didn't want me, the Dixon's used me, Matron Flagg hates me, and the Murrays want you until they change their mind all together and don't want you at all! Rodney's gone too! Now you! And what I am supposed to make of this?"

"Trust me, I know what it's like to feel abandoned–"

"They didn't abandon me, Bill, they didn't leave. They *sent* me away. There's a difference." Coral flung her arms about the compartment. "I didn't do any of this. Any of it. I just got caught up in other people's shit, and I'm the one who suffers. Me and Rodney. None of this was my fault, yet I'm the one everyone blames and punishes. And you're supposed to make it all better?"

The compartment door slid open, and the conductor noted the young man on the floor and the hysterical woman sobbing into her handkerchief. "Is everything alright in here, young lady?"

Coral nodded and sniffed.

Bill took a seat next to Coral, put his arm around her and encouraged her to rest her head on his shoulder.

And so, they sat in silence for quite a while, until Bill squeezed her closer.

"You know what the opposite of being unwanted is?"

Coral shook her head. "It's being sought after. You're worth being sought after, and we'll show Rodney he is, too. Together?"

Coral nodded gently. "Together. Alright then."

Thursday 15th September, 1949—
C.W.D. Flinders Street Railway Building

Bill and Coral held hands and trotted along the grey footpath of Flinders Street.

"They'll think we're being stupid and impulsive," Coral said.

"Just stick to the story. Mrs Hutchinson said she'd back us up."

"What if they don't believe us?"

"We keep at them until they do."

Coral let go and twisted the ring on her finger to its correct position. "We're not even doing it right. Wish we could've found my dad."

"You know what, Coral? Whenever I imagined proposing to a girl, never once did it cross my mind, I'd have to ask an entire department for permission. We're not doing anything right, and that's what makes our story ours."

Department Report

Girl accompanied by her fiancée, William King, 20 years, called.

They are desirous of being married. King is an orphan. He is employed at McIlwraith Brass Moulders and he resides at Dickmann St, Richmond. He is in receipt of 7 pound, 6 shillings per week exclusive of overtime.

He has been engaged to Coral for the last three months, during which time he has accompanied her at her visits to her child. He states he is prepared to regard this child as his own.

Both he and Coral are emphatic that there is no urgent reason for their marriage. They state that they are aware of their responsibilities, and if they are permitted to marry, they will reside in a house at Sunbury. This property is owned by King's brother.

William King has been offered a good situation at Sunshine Cabinet Makers. Though young, he appears to be a sensible type, and perhaps the proposed marriage would be the best future for Coral.

CONSENT TO MARRIAGE OF WARD OF CHILDREN'S WELFARE DEPARTMENT
MARRIAGE ACT 1928 SECTION 40 (1)b.

I, EDWARD JAMES DOBSON, Secretary of the Children's Welfare Department, Melbourne, hereby consent to the marriage of my ward CORAL MAXWELL, born 13/9/30, residing at Roseberry Street, Ascot Vale, with WILLIAM KING residing at Dickmann Street, Richmond.

Signed at Melbourne this 19th day of September, 1949

To the Future

1949

Saturday 8th October, 1949—
Union Hotel, Union Road, Ascot Vale

Bill grabbed the beer crate from the barman and stepped onto it. He knew most of the people who'd gathered in the pub lounge. There were workmates, friends, and family among the faces who were waiting for the mystery announcement he'd promised them.

Bill raised a glass of beer. "Everyone charged?"

A chorus of approval sounded.

"This beautiful girl next to me, Coral, has agreed to become my wife!"

Cheers erupted and faces popped in from the public bar to see what the fuss was about.

Bill continued. "Now I want you all to make sure you keep the date free."

"Good timing," someone called. "We might turn up now the footy season's over."

Once the laughter settled, Bill spoke again. "Now, this part is a surprise for Coral too. You see, I went and spoke to the minister this morning, and we'll be getting hitched on the 22nd!"

Coral grasped his arm, "I can't get ready in two weeks!"

Bill winked at her. "Sure you can, love"

A loud voice spoke above the commotion. "Oh, so there's a reason for a speedy ceremony, then?"

"Not the kind you think." Bill corrected them. "We're going down to collect little Rodney as soon as we can."

A sea of glasses raised in the air in front of Bill and Coral. "To Rodney!" they called.

"Well, our Bill's quick off the mark, isn't he? His family's come ready-made!"

"To Bill and Coral!"

So many voices wished them well, even shouts from the public bar, and the bartender raised his glass as well.

Bill stepped from his perch into a flurry of handshakes, backslaps, and shouts[1] of Fosters[2].

The women surrounded Coral to offer congratulatory hugs and admire her engagement ring. "So where are you getting married?" one asked.

"That pretty little church on the hill in Richmond."

"St Stephens?"

"Yes, that's the one."

She laughed. "Well, Bill better not be late; it's only a couple of blocks from his house."

---

1. Another pays on your behalf

2. Brand of beer

Saturday 22nd October, 1949— St Stephens Anglican Church, Richmond

As soon as Coral's eyes blinked open, she leapt from her bed and pulled the curtains apart. Her bedroom window looked upon the narrow path that ran up the side of Lorna's house and most of the side fence. She tipped her head sideways to get a good look at the sky. Not clear, but no heavy clouds either. It seemed fitting that today offered her unsettled weather. One minute bright and sunny, the next threatening to rain; it matched her nerves perfectly.

The car was new, beautiful and cream and arrived right on time. Mrs Hutchinson had made a call to her friends at the Widow's Society, and it turned out one of their son's had just purchased a car and would love to drive for the bride.

"Watch the veil! Watch the veil!" Mrs Hutchinson's worried orders had everyone on edge.

"I've got it, Mrs Hutchinson," Allison called over her shoulder. "Please relax a little. You'll do yourself an injury." Allison winked at Coral as she slid into the backseat beside her.

Mrs Hutchinson made her way around to the driver's side and tapped at his window until he wound it down. "Make sure you wait here a while. Oh, and drive slowly; the bride must be a few minutes late."

The driver lifted his hat. "Of course, Mrs Hutchinson." He then checked the girls were okay in the back and offered them a roll of his eyes.

"Now girls," she continued," I'll meet you at the church." She strode across the road to where Lorna and another relative with a car were waiting. "Deep breaths Coral, deep breaths."

Allison giggled. "Sheesh, has she even taken one herself this morning?"

"She's done an amazing job to get everything ready in time."

Allison slid her hand along the car's new upholstery. "That woman can rummage up anything, can't she? And you! Just look at you."

"The department released all my money to me this week. Thank God they gave me money for my dress, before then."

Coral took a deep breath and let it out slowly. Almost there. Almost a married woman, and getting prepared sped by in a blur.

Lorna's garden looked sweet this morning. Some of her pansies had bloomed, and there were more buds on the way. But Coral wouldn't be coming back tonight. She wouldn't be here tomorrow to see which buds had blossomed.

Allison nudged Coral and nodded to Mrs Hutchinson's car turning onto Union Road, "Hope she packed enough hankies."

Coral laughed. "I can't believe how much she cried this morning."

"She cried when the florist brought the carnations to you."

"You should have seen her when I first tried on the dress!"

The girls laughed and adjusted each other's hair, making sure everything was just so.

"Ready ladies?" their driver asked and started the car.

The girls held hands and rested them on Coral's satin skirt. "Ready."

"Best of luck to you, love." The driver kissed Coral's hand. She'd managed to make it out of the car without falling over and now stood in the shadow of the imposing bluestone church that rose behind the short iron fence. She breathed deeply again. Mrs Hutchinson was right. The deep breaths did help when her nerves got the better of her. Allison mumbled something, but the thought that her future lay just beyond the double gothic doors distracted Coral.

"C'mon Coral, no use standing there with your mouth open."

Allison guided her through the gate, and Coral's head tugged backward sharply. "The veil!" she cried.

Allison quickly untangled it from the iron spires along the fence. "There's only a small rip."

"A rip?"

"A tear, actually; no, not even a tear, a hole, a small hole, that's what I mean."

"I've torn it?" Coral's eyes stung with tears.

"No. I mean, yes you have, but it's a good thing. It's a good thing." Allison tidied the veil and put her arm around Coral's shoulder. "It's very lucky to tear your dress or your veil on your wedding day."

"It is?"

"Absolutely. One of the best signs of good luck and a happy future. And I should know, right? I've done this before."

Coral had calmed down by the time they reached the doors. "Thanks Allison."

"You're welcome. Everything all right?"

Coral wiggled her shoe. "The sixpence Mrs Hutchinson put in there is stuck to the ball of my foot."

"You can show me the imprint later," she smiled, and kissed her on the cheek. The organ music drifted from the church through the doors. "They're ready for us. I'm off first. Meet you at the end of the aisle."

Coral nodded; her mouth suddenly too dry to speak.

Coral stood at the beginning of the aisle, squeezing the carnation spray in her hands. Her legs had wobbled a bit when she took her place, but now she stood tall. The polished wooden pews held their collective friends and family, and Bill stood smiling at the altar.

The minister was quite happy for her to walk herself down the aisle. He said it was becoming quite common these days, what with the war and everything.

In many ways, it felt right.

She was the one who'd done all the hard work to get to this moment.

She's practically raised herself, and she certainly didn't feel like the property of someone to be given away.

She'd had enough of that.

She was done with rules and feeling powerless.

She was choosing herself, she was choosing Rodney, and she was choosing Bill.

She was choosing her own life for the very first time.

It was terrifying, but it was a good kind of terrifying.

The minister's wife, Helen, watched from the organ, and waited for Coral's brief nod to signal she was ready. Coral didn't care what was played, as long as she made it to Bill waiting at the end of the aisle.

The strains of *Jesu, Joy of Man's Desiring*, began. Coral counted to five, and took her first steps into her new life. The one she chose with all her heart.

Saturday 24th December, 1949—Dawson Street, Sunshine

Carols played on the little wireless in the lounge room, and Rodney was fast asleep in his bedroom. Coral snuggled into Bill on the old couch a kind neighbour had given to them. "This is my best Christmas ever."

"It's not even Christmas yet."

"It will be tomorrow. So, I think it counts as tonight as well."

Bill thought for a while. "I think it's my best Christmas too. Made even better by the best Christmas tree in Melbourne."

"Melbourne? I thought you said it was the best Christmas tree in the world."

"I'm just trying to be humble."

But it *was* the best Christmas tree in the world.

Like 'the best' of anything, it came with its own story and memory. It didn't matter that it was a branch ripped off a gum tree in the local park, or that Bill had carried it for ten minutes before he realised a policeman was following them, and by then they were almost home. The constable had given Bill a firm warning about destroying public property, then helped him bring it through the door. It still remained on the disastrous lean it was set to on the afternoon it arrived, and was decorated as best as they could with linked newspaper chains. The highlight was the angel with the tip of its wing broken off, that arrived in the letterbox the day after the tree arrived.

"It *is* the best Christmas tree in the world though," Coral smiled.

"All ready for tomorrow?"

"I'm looking forward to catching up with Alex and Allison."
"Allison makes a bonza[3] roast too. You'll love it."
"I have a little gift for you tomorrow too."
"You do? And tell me Mrs King, will you be on Santa's naughty or nice list?"
"It doesn't matter. I've got everything I need already."

<u>Monday 20th March, 1950—Dawson Street, Sunshine</u>

It was a warm morning for March, one of those days where the patchy sky didn't know whether it wanted to rain or not. Coral took nearly two-year-old Rodney outside into the fresh air to play. Who knew what the afternoon would bring? The front garden had softer grass for his little feet, and he liked to use cups to water the plants that grew along the short concrete path that led to the front door.

Coral rested on the porch chair and watched Rodney toddle back and forth across the garden, stopping to investigate snails, rocks, plants, and whatever caught his fancy.

"Fwower mummy!" Rodney placed a bent but carefully picked dandelion in Coral's face for her admiration.

"That's a dandelion. You watch mummy." Coral's puff blew the seeds all over the small lawn. Rodney thought the whole idea hilarious and ran off and brought her a blade of grass to do it again.

The blast from the postman's whistle made Rodney jump, and he made it to the fence and the all-important letterbox at the same time as the postman.

The postman lifted his hat to Coral and adjusted his mailbag. "Good morning Mrs. King."

"Good morning."

---

3. Terrific

Rodney waddled toward her with an envelope in his hand. "Mummy mail" he announced.

"Thank you, postman Rodney."

The envelope looked official. Coral squinted into the morning sun as she ripped the top of the envelope and pulled the letter out.

<u>Wednesday 15th March, 1950</u>
The abovementioned ward is now discharged from her wardship.
By order of the Secretary,
Children's Welfare Department

Rodney toddled past, and Coral swept him up into a big hug and landed kisses on his cheeks. "Thank you, Rodney. That's the best news ever!"

Coral rubbed at her rounded belly and tipped her face to the sun. In her mind's eye, the flutter of every dandelion wish ever made, had finally arrived home.

The End

Afterword

Albert Francis Maxwell didn't contact his children on his return from the war.

Two years after his discharge in 1945, he married for the second time.

Perhaps it was his drive for a new life that led him to deny that he had any previous children.

In 1968, when he was 64 years old, Albert Maxwell succumbed to bowel cancer at his home in Collingwood.

There are no children listed on his death certificate.

Allan Maxwell, Coral's eldest brother was fortunate enough to find a long-term foster home. He grew up in a stable and loving home in the suburb of Springvale South and worked as a mechanic.

Ronald Maxwell, the youngest of Coral's brothers, remained at the Berwick Boys Home until his release from the department at 18. He worked in the shoemaker/bootmaker trade. Ronald married and settled at Thomastown, where he lived until his death in 2012.

Rodney Maxwell-King, Coral's first child, died in a car accident in March 1965. He was travelling with friends to Sale, when the driver lost control and the car rolled. Rodney was 16 years old and the only fatality.

Dudley William King (Bill), and Coral were married for 28 years. Bill died at the age of 48 after a battle with Hodgkin's Lymphoma. His death in 1977 created a new role for Coral, that of single mother to their remaining nine children. Seven of which, were still at home.

Coral May Maxwell-King passed away from lung cancer in May 2006. She spent her final days at home, surrounded and supported by her family. She lived a hard life, one that featured a great amount of loss and grief, but also an incredible amount of the love and admiration that was denied to her as a child. Regardless of what life threw at her, Coral remained tender hearted and an example to us all.

Wife to Dudley William (Bill)
Mother to 10 children, their friends and partners.
Grandmother to 27
Great grandmother to 49
Great-great grandmother to 5
(2023)

Rest in peace Coral. We are all so very proud of you.

Author Note

Thank you for reading *'Dandelion Wishes'*. I hope you enjoyed Coral's story and are as inspired by her determination as I was when discovering her life's tale.

You can find selected family photos at www.lisakingauthor.com/dandelion-wishes-photos

I truly appreciate the feedback I get from my readers. If you enjoy my work, please consider leaving a review at your store of purchase, or on review sites such as Goodreads.

Reviews not only help other readers find books they might enjoy, they can also be instrumental in a book's success.

Word-of-Mouth is always the best way to find books you like, so please share your thoughts about *'Dandelion Wishes'* among friends and family and don't forget to share on social media.

Thank you!

Acknowledgements

Books don't appear from thin air. They are a collaborative effort, whether in support or deed, and my heartfelt thanks go to every person involved in this project.

Firstly, to Coral, for inspiring us all.

To my sister-in-law, Sylvia Riley-King for continuing Coral's dream of tracing her family. Without her tenacity and hours spent in front of the computer chasing down defunct state departments, we would still be in the dark as to Coral's story.

To Stewart, who gets dragged from pillar to post on all my investigations, and listens to me waffle on at all hours of the day and night. My beloved patron who allows me to continue the work I love the most.

To the many people I interviewed, telephoned, or allowed access to their websites. The people who photocopied, called, texted and sent photos. Those who let us rummage through their databases and welcomed us into the homes, offices, and schools.

To the archivists who keep our histories safe and alive, and to the historians and journalists who painted eloquent pictures through their words so we might better understand times gone by.

To the wider spread of global information via google/google maps and Trove Newspapers and the Trove Volunteers.

To the private Facebook Groups that graciously welcomed me in and answered my strange questions. To the National Library of Australia, ancestry.com, and PROV-Public Record Office Victoria.

Without you, this book would not exist in this form.
With special thanks to-

Fitzroy

Melbourne Metropolitan Board of Works
Fitzroy Historical Society

Parkville

C.L.A.N Care Leavers Network
Find and Connect
Forgotten Australians
Shurlee Swain
Australian Military Records
Kev Blacker

Children's Welfare Department of Victoria

Ward records
Department of Health and Human Services – Victoria

Our Station – Flinders Street

Carlton

Carlton Community History Group
Trove Newspapers

East Kew Girls Home/Catherine Booth Home for Girls

Shirley Steans
Salvation Army Museum
All the Home girls – survivors and sisters
'Time behind the Green Door' by Shirley Steans
'A Window of Time' by Shirley Steans

Jeetho

Eric Thorpe
Carol Thorpe
Korumburra and District Historical Society Inc.
Libby Lambert
'History of the Shire of Korumburra' by Joseph White
'Reflections of Jeetho' by Lorraine Knox (ed.)

Mt Evelyn

Mt Evelyn History Group
Paula Herlihy
Karen Phillips
Janice Newton
Lilydale and District Historical Society Inc.
Sue Thompson

Spring House

Salvation Army Museum
Gillian Giles
Trove Newspapers

City Mission Maternity Home

Hartnett House
Brunswick Community History Group Inc.
MCM Early Years Hub
'*Hartnett House, Brunswick. Its Founder, Its Work, Its History.*' by Banda Dagher
'*Sister Elizabeth Hartnett: a Woman of Beneficence.*' by Banda Dagher

Nhill

Nhill and District Historical Society
Colleen Forbes

Ascot Vale

Essendon Historical Society
Herbert Adams Pty Ltd

Richmond

St Stephens Anglican Church
Richmond and Burnley Historical Society

Huge and heartfelt thanks to my incredible Beta Team, whose solace, advice, and tidbits of information helped pull this book together.

Jen Bartlett
Kev Blacker
Michelle Capper
Kass Hall
Lauren King
Jayne Meon
Heather Musingo
Siobhan Pope
Sylvia Riley-King
Joanne Smith

                Thank You.

About the Author

Lisa King is a international award winning author and amateur nature photographer who lives near Brisbane, Australia. When she's not writing, you can find her hiking though lush rainforests, and exploring the wide open spaces of the Scenic Rim, taking notes for her novels and capturing the diverse and complex ecosystems where she feels most at home.

Lisa loves to transport readers to worlds where the heroes have everyday struggles, flaws and inner conflicts, and the natural world is part of the nurturing and healing process. As an advocate for education and empathy for trauma survivors, Lisa hopes her books will encourage readers on their own healing paths.

Visit her website, www.lisakingauthor.com to join her *'Readers Circle'*, a monthly newsletter with all her goings on, and a few gifts along the way! You can connect with Lisa via email (lisa@lisakingauthor.com), and find her on social media, as Lisa King Author.

AWENMELL SERIES
Crown of Fire – Awenmell Series : Book One
Rise – Awenmell Series : Book Two

AWENMELL CHARACTER SERIES
Magic Man – Awenmell Characters 1
Eshnae – Awenmell Characters 2

STANDALONES
Dandelion Wishes – The Untold Story of Coral Maxwell King

www.ingramcontent.com/pod-product-compliance
Lightning Source LLC
Chambersburg PA
CBHW030251010526
44107CB00053B/1661